The Wise Guy and the Fool

A Philosophical Odyssey from Modern Error to Truth

Matthew D'Antuono

En Route Books and Media, LLC
5705 Rhodes Avenue
St. Louis, MO 63109

Cover credit: TJ Burdick

Library of Congress Control Number: 2018914873

ISBN-13: 978-1-950108-00-8
ISBN-10: 1-950108-00-7

Alternative Titles for this Book

An Attempt to Popularize Profundities
or
Sarcasm at the Service of Philosophy
or
Philosophy for People with ADD
or
A Philosopher's use of Rhetoric
or
Philosophical Conversations and Short Stories
or
The Wisdom of Common Sense
or
What Happens When an Amateur Philosopher and Writer Tries to Write a Book
or
In Defense of Common-Sensism
or
Extrapolations of Common Sense
or
Why I am a Catholic
or
Thomistic Entertainment

There are two kinds of people in the world: the fools who think that they are wise, and the wise who know that they are fools.

– Peter Kreeft

About the Author and This Book

It has come to the author's attention that people reading this book might like to know something about him. He would like to begin simply by pointing out that he does not pretend to know it all or be perfect. He is more of a constant student of philosophy than an expert in it, and he is daily and sometimes hourly reminded of his human weakness in the face of any trial. He is the father of seven children who are always assisting him in his efforts to know himself better. Therefore, he is in constant need of the grace, mercy, and love of God, in Whom he places his trust and hope.

As for his qualifications for writing this book, he holds bachelor's degrees in physics and philosophy and is at work on a master's in philosophy. He works as a high school physics teacher, so he spends a lot of time thinking about how to convey abstract ideas in understandable ways.

If there are any errors in the pages that follow, they may be attributed to the author; of the timeless truths entailed, he is at best a transmitter, a conduit, or a translator (as you can see, redundancy is one of his strengths). He has never had a truly original thought in his life, and he now tires of typing about himself in the third person.

Some people have something worth saying, but they never say it; others don't have anything worth saying, but they just keep saying it. I hope to have escaped both categories, but I leave it to the reader to decide.

What follows is not a textbook on philosophy. It is not an essay on philosophy. It is not a treatise on philosophy. It is more like philosophical entertainment and illustration: a collection of philosophical dialogues, allegories, stories, and explanations. They are arranged according to chapters that begin with a critique of some of the dominant but wholly irrational ideas in the world today and end with a recognition of the source of highest truth, which man is unable to attain on his own.

The illustrations were crafted by Br. François, CFR, of the Franciscan Friars of the Renewal. I am a Lay Associate of the Friars, which means that I make an effort to help the friars in their work with the poor. I am only a tiny little bit less than certain that they have helped me far more than I have been able to help them.

Acknowledgments

The debt of gratitude can never be paid in full, but here is an attempt to repay at least a small part of it.

Thank you to my wife, who is always a source of inspiration and comfort to me.

Thank you to Dr. Sebastian Mahfood, OP, for agreeing to work with me on this project and giving me the suggestion to find an illustrator.

Thank you to Br. François, CFR, for his amazing illustrations; it has been a unique delight to see my meagerly imagined ideas brought to life with such vivid detail and personality.

Thank you to Fr. John-Mary, CFR, and to Dr. Timothy Smith for reading a draft of the manuscript and offering helpful guidance.

And since I agree wholeheartedly with Carl Sagan's statement that "If you want to make an apple pie from scratch, you have to first create the universe," I would like to thank my Lord and Savior, Jesus Christ, through Whom all things were made.

There are many more people (in Heaven and on Earth) to whom I owe thanks, and I offer to them my apologies for not including their names here.

Stuff in this Book
(Table of Contents)

Chapter 1: Popular Ideas that Don't Make Much Sense 1

Chapter 2: The Illusion of Illusions, the mistake of mistakes 11

Excursus on Pride vs. Humility 21

Chapter 3: How to be Certain about Certainty 27

Chapter 4: Iconoclasm of Science-Worship ... 45

Chapter 5: Hidden in Plain Sight 55

Chapter 6: What Kinds of Things are Things? 67

Chapter 7: What Makes Man a Man? 79

Chapter 8: Right Makes Right 93

Chapter 9: The Real Theory of Everything ... 101

Chapter 10: The God-Man 117

Chapter 11: The Pillar and Bulwark of the Truth 127

A Philosophical Sermon on the Meaning of Life 143

Why You Should Not Have Read This Book . 153

Chapter 1

Popular Ideas that Don't Make Much Sense

T or F?

1. There is no truth.

2. You believe what you want to believe and I will believe what I want to believe.

3. Truth is relative.

4. Whether or not this statement is true is a matter of opinion.

I am aware that the first three statements are part of the air that we breathe as a society. We are concerned about offending people, an admirable sentiment, but we have thrown the baby out with the bath water. In an effort to be more accepting of people, we have thrown away the belief in true ideas. As we try to establish more social sanity, we have given way to some mental insanity. It makes all the sense in the world to embrace people no matter what their beliefs, but it makes no sense at all to say that all beliefs are equally true or false.

There is one statement with which we must all agree: there is such a thing as truth. First of all, if there were no truth, then the very statement "There is no truth" could not be true. If truth were relative, then the statement "Truth is relative" would also have to be relative.

Every statement, in the end, is either true or false; in other words fact or fiction. The "fact vs opinion" dichotomy is false. An opinion is nothing more than a weak form of knowledge, an idea someone holds but does not have much good reason for believing. For most people, the idea that the earth is in motion is mere opinion because they do not know it for themselves. But the statement that the earth is in motion is either fact or fiction.

For anyone embarking on the arduous but fascinating journey of philosophy, it must be clear from the start that truth is real. The word philosophy means love of wisdom. If there is no wisdom to be had, no insight into truth and the nature of reality, then philosophy must be abandoned and so must every other discipline.

Wiseguy: Ok, then. What is truth?

Fool: Well, I think that if I say something that matches the way things really are, then it is true. If I have an idea that does not match the way things really are, then it's false. I don't see how it could be any other way.

Wiseguy: But what makes a statement true?

Fool: It just is if it really describes the reality of something. Like if I say that the page is white and the page is white in reality. That is an example of a true statement.

Wiseguy: But what if your reality is different from my reality.

Fool: Then I think that makes us all crazy.

Two men enter a bar. They order two drinks.

"Hello friend! How are you today?"

"Your today or my today?"

"Your today."

"I am doing well in my today. Although, now I think we are in your today."

The bartender pours the drinks.

"No, I don't think so. In my reality liquids go up when released from their containers. These liquids are not going up," he says as he spills his drink to see what happens.

"Oh, that's new! Why did you make that change?"

"I wanted to try something different, so I changed the physical laws of my universe. I am going to have to change them again. It is not working out too well. I think an implosion is immanent." Nodding towards the liquid, "This must mean that we are in your reality."

"No, I don't think so. Liquids fall down in my reality."

The spilled drink had not gone down or up but remains in a blob where it left the glass.

The bartender speaks up. “This is my reality. It’s easier to clean up.”

“Oh,” say both men as they nod their heads in agreement. “Cheers!”

A woman walking down the street in New York City loudly proclaims to all that she is the queen of the Andromeda Galaxy, and all must bow to her or she will freeze them with her alien powers. She brandishes a twig at the passersby. When they do not bow down, she points the stick at them and makes a loud whooshing noise, as if she were casting a spell or shooting them with some invisible energy. When they ignore her, she tackles them. Police arrest her, and she is placed in an insane asylum. It is said amongst the doctors that she is out of touch with reality. The queen of Andromeda rages in her cell throughout the night, “It’s true for me!”

Wiseguy: Nothing exists.

Fool: Well, if that’s true, then you and I don’t exist. That thing you just said doesn’t exist either then, right?

Wiseguy: Yes. My statement does not exist.

Fool: I’m confused. How can you make it, or how can I hear it, or how can we talk about it if it doesn’t exist?

Wiseguy: It is an illusion.

Fool: What does "it is" even mean?

Wiseguy: It is a figment of our consciousness.

Fool: If nothing exists, does your consciousness exist?

Wiseguy: No.

Fool: So, something that does not exist can think, have consciousness, and have illusions?

Wiseguy: Yes.

Why do people who believe that nothing really exists, that everything is merely an illusion, eat breakfast?

Shouldn't people who think that they are the only thing that exists commit themselves to an insane asylum since they admit that they are seeing and experiencing things that do not really exist?

Idea: We all just have our own experiences, but there is no objective reality.

Problem with the idea: There is no such thing as an empty experience; we have only experiences of things.

Solution: Those experiences are experiences of reality. The experiences are individual and subjective. The reality is common and objective. The idea is wrong.

"Welcome to the open-mindedness club. Let's introduce ourselves. My name is open-minded Omar."

"Hi, Omar."

"My name is relativity Ralph, and I am somewhere else."

"Hi, Ralph."

"My name is subjective Sam, and I am not a human."

"Hi, Sam."

Omar chimes in, "And I see we have a newcomer tonight. Why don't you tell us your name?"

"Um. Hi. My name is Chris. My friends think I am too closed-minded, and they heard about this group. So, they suggested I come here."

"Welcome."

Omar takes the lead again. "Welcome. The format of this meeting is that we listen to what everyone has to say and practice being open-minded. So, let us open our minds." Omar, Ralph, and Sam grab the tops of their heads and lift up to expose their empty skulls. Chris also removes the top of his head, but his brain is still taking up that precious space. "Who would like to begin?" Ralph and Sam both raise their hands. "Ralph, why don't you start us off." Ralph waits and looks at Sam. "Ralph, you can begin," repeats Omar.

Ralph, as if waking up, says, "I was waiting for Sam to begin."

"But I called on you," rejoins Omar.

"That might be true for you, but for me it's true that you called on Sam," returns Ralph.

"Very clever! How interesting. Can't be closed-minded about that. He heard what he heard, and there can be no denying it," come the compliments from both Omar and Sam.

Chris sheepishly interposes, "But, Omar clearly called on Ralph. What are you guys talking about?"

Omar answers, "No need to be so judgmental! You are not being very open-minded." Chris looks puzzled, sits back in his chair, and folds his arms; classic closed-minded body language. "What would you like to share today, Ralph?"

"Well, I would like to say that I have invented a new religion."

"Fantastic! We love new religions!"

"Yes, yes," says Ralph, holding his hand up to calm the crowd. "In this religion I worship my big toe."

"Splendid! You've really done it now."

"I have decided that I don't have a big toe."

"Why?" says Chris loudly, putting a damper on the excited mood in the room.

"Because I want to," replies Ralph. "Do you have any idea how important the big toe is? If we didn't have a big toe, we wouldn't be able to balance, and we'd be falling over all the time."

"That's what he thinks! How progressive and creative," cheer Omar and Sam.

"Yes, and in this religion I paint my big toe nails every week and I wrap my big toes in gauze every night before bed so they are snug."

Chris sits now in a state of semi-astonishment, and it is obvious to the other members. Sam brings his big hand down on Chris's back with a thud and says, "Don't look so surprised. This is good for you. It is healthy and freeing to be more open-minded." However, Chris barely hears a word of Sam's little pep-talk. Sam is a large, strong man, and the pat on the back that is meant to encourage poor Chris knocks the brain out of his head. As Sam is talking, Chris is just getting used to a very new and different feeling.

Omar continues, "Who else would like to share." Chris enthusiastically raises his hand. Happy to see the newcomer willing to talk, Omar calls on Chris.

"My name is craniotomy Chris, and I will never make another judgment again." A blissful smile spreads across Chris's face as the words fall from his mouth.

"Now we are getting somewhere! That's real progress. Tell it the way you want it to be," call out the rest of the group.

Once we know that objective reality exists, the goal for any rational being (e.g. a human being) is to find out what objective reality is like. Man by nature desires to know. Therefore, when we seek to invent reality or ignore truth, we are not living up to our nature as humans. If humans desire truth by nature, then those who do not desire truth are not realizing their full potential.

Chapter 2

The Illusion of Illusions, the Mistake of Mistakes

T or F?
1. Everything is an illusion.
2. People make mistakes.
3. People cannot know reality because they make mistakes.
4. There is no way to tell if you are awake or asleep right now.

There is no getting around reality. Either it is there (or here), or everything is an illusion. However, in order for there to be illusion in the first place, there must be some reality to be mistaken about, and there must be someone to experience the illusion.

A man walks into a dimly lit bar and sees a man wearing a pink shirt and begins laughing at him.

"Why are you laughing at me?"

"Because you are wearing a pink shirt."

"I am not."

"Yes, you are."

"Let's take this outside."

It is the end of June, when the days are long, so the sun is still out. In the brighter light, the shirt no longer looks pink but white.

"You see? My shirt is not pink, but white."

"Alas! I can no longer trust any of my sense perceptions! I will never know what reality is actually like!"

Both men return to the bar and have a drink.

Wiseguy: People can't really know anything because they make mistakes.

Fool: People make mistakes? How do you know?

Wiseguy: Because they come to some conclusion and then later find out that their initial conclusion was wrong.

Fool: How do they know that their initial conclusion was wrong?

Wiseguy: Because they check again, or someone corrects them.

Fool: But you just said that people can't really know anything. If they can't know anything, how can they learn that they were mistaken? Doesn't the fact that we make mistakes depend on there actually being a right answer and that we can know the right answer? If we can't know the right answer, we can't know that we make mistakes.

A first grade class.

Teacher: Johnny, what is ten plus fifteen?

Johnny: There is no way to know. All of reality is an illusion.

Teacher: Incorrect.

Wiseguy: I saw a TV special that proved how unreliable the human memory is.

Fool: Does that mean your memory of the TV special is unreliable? If our memories are so bad, how can you be sure that you saw a TV special on how bad the memory is?

There once was a man who locked himself up inside of his own head, that impenetrable and inescapable prison of insanity and really bad ideas. This mental institution has since been willingly entered by many a modern philosopher, all bent on the destruction of that fortress, all seeking the secret passageway out, however convoluted and serpentine the crawl might be. Most have succeeded only in creating imaginary realities that are shoved and stuffed into the already crowded cell. Others have reached the point of despair, but, having forgotten that they were the creators of their own surroundings, gave up.

This fascinating feat of self-deception was accomplished by denying everything that could be questioned and throwing by the wayside anything that was not immediately self-evident. By reducing philosophy to logic and epistemology to mathematics, by looking for a kind of certainty that was beyond the scope of the discipline, by employing methods alien to the subject, these men have lost themselves in the labyrinth of apprehension, sensation, and judgment.

The point of philosophy is to attain truth, the correspondence of thought and reality. If our philosophy is leading us further and further from reality, further and further from those data which are most immediate and obvious, it is time to consider a different philosophy.

There once was a man who used mathematics to describe nature. He assigned certain values and systems of measurement to various quantities he observed. After doing some math, he found that by mere algebra and simple arithmetic, he could predict the outcome of many events. He continued to apply these principles until he could make predictions about things beyond his everyday experience, things too small or too far away to perceive directly, and he got some very strange results. These things do not behave like things that he could perceive directly. However, by this time, he forgot that the math was only a description of quantities, measurements of certain characteristics of the objects, not the objects themselves.

He then made the mistake of trying to mathematicise all things, even in philosophy. That was like asking a lover to define his beloved, like asking a girl who had lived among horses her whole life to define one, and what ought never to have been confined by definition in the first place was reduced to a mere description. Some philosophers have become so caught up in their ideas of things that they have lost touch with the things themselves; they have become so obsessed with knowing the description of reality that they have come to care nothing for knowing reality itself.

A man is not the sum of his statistics.

Skepticism hacks away at the boulder of common sense with a plastic knife. Not making much progress, he starts walking around to the other side where he meets Scientism (i.e. (Latin for *id est* (*id est*: that is (that is to say (in other words))))) science worship).

"Hello, Scientism, my friend. What are you doing here?"

"Oh, I am just trying to tear down this boulder. You?"

"Same. I am not getting very far very fast with this plastic knife, but if I keep at it, the boulder will eventually wear down."

"Yeah. This plastic spoon is not doing much for me either."

They both begin hacking, cutting, and scooping at the boulder again.

"So, where did you get that spoon?"

"Oh, as a result of our experiments. We have learned that all our perceptions are an illusion."

"Yeah, I agree."

"It took a lot of time, a lot of observations, reading data, analyzing, but we finally came to the conclusion that..."

"Wait...did you say observations? Reading data?" Skepticism looks surprised.

"Yeah, why?" replies scientism.

"Well, I don't think we can trust the senses."

"Right, neither do I."

"But you were just talking about observations and data." Skepticism is now confused.

"Right. And?"

"What do you use to make those observations?"

Scientism stands like a deer caught in the headlights. Skepticism slowly backs away.

I ought to doubt every statement that I cannot prove.

I cannot prove that I ought to doubt every statement that I cannot prove.

Therefore, I ought to doubt that I ought to doubt every statement that I cannot prove.

i.e. The skeptic ought to be skeptical about skepticism.

"What is your philosophy?"

"I am a skeptic."

"Why not be skeptical about being a skeptic? How are you sure you are a skeptic?"

"Because I believe that we should not make any assumptions. We should begin with doubt."

"Isn't it an assumption to assume that we ought to begin with doubt? Why not doubt that we should begin with doubt?"

Wiseguy: How do you know you are not sleeping right now?

Fool: Because I know that I am awake.

Wiseguy: How do you know you are awake?

Fool: Because I know what it is like to be awake.

Wiseguy: How do you know what it is like to be awake?

Fool: Because I have experienced being awake.

Wiseguy: How do you know you have experienced being awake?

Fool: Because I have also fallen asleep, and woken up, and dreamt, and I can tell the difference between those experiences.

Wiseguy: How can you tell the difference?

Fool: The quality of the experience. Something is different.

Wiseguy: But how can you really know for sure?

Fool: Well, I can't prove it in a mathematical way, but all the evidence points to the fact that I am awake. There is no evidence that I am asleep.

An apple is placed before a man. Tell us, oh man, what you see in front of you.

"I see an apple."

Is it truly an apple?

The man leans in and squints as he looks at it. He moves to one side, eyeing the fruit carefully. "Yes."

But, are you really sure?

The man looks at us and furrows his brow. He turns back to the apple. He picks it up, smells it, takes a bite of it. "Yes, I am really sure."

Why?

"Because I can see it, touch it, taste it, smell it."

Can you be sure that you are not imagining it?

"Yup. I can be pretty sure of that."

Maybe it is all just a dream!

"No. I am not sleeping right now."

Maybe you are just seeing things!

"No. That is definitely an apple in front of me."

Prove it!

"I get the feeling you are looking for some

sort of proof that I can't give."

Aha! Then you don't really know!

"No, I know. I just know in the way we know most things, not in the way we know things in abstract logical systems. This is knowledge of reality, based on experience, not mathematics which based on axioms."

Doubting everything is the opposite but equally lazy and dangerous mistake as believing everything. The hard work of thinking, evaluating, and judging is avoided.

It is true that people make mistakes, but that does not mean that no knowledge is possible. It only means that we need to further investigate our initial perceptions, thoughts, and conclusions by reviewing them and checking them with other people. Lack of infallibility does not imply complete lack of certainty. Our experience and knowledge of reality does not rely on pristine and indubitable axioms, but on our senses, memories, perceptions, and interactions.

Excursus on Pride vs. Humility

Pride: the attitude of the mind that seeks to create its own reality and is unwilling to accept evidence and reason, wherever it comes from.

Humility: the attitude of the mind that is willing to accept an accurate appraisal of reality.

Pride:
"Nice job on that report, Sanders!"
"Well, I really wasn't comfortable with the results I got. I don't think it was really that great."

Humility:
"Nice job on that report, Sanders!"
"Thank you."

Pride:

I know you just proved me wrong, and that all the evidence stands against my belief, but I still think I am right. I just haven't figured out how to word my beliefs correctly.

Humility:

After listening to your argument and seeing that the evidence lies against my prior belief, I am changing my mind.

Pride:

"Thank you for your help, Sanders."

"Oh, it was nothing. I didn't really do much."

Humility:

"Thank you for your help, Sanders."

"You're welcome."

Pride: I really do not have a problem with ________________ [choose from: alcohol, marijuana, cocaine, gambling, pornography, technology, stealing, overeating, prostitutes, video games, hoarding, shopping, ...], and I can stop whenever I want.

Humility: I really am powerless over ________________ [choose from: alcohol, marijuana, cocaine, gambling, pornography, technology, stealing, overeating, prostitutes, video games, hoarding, shopping, ...], my life has become unmanageable, and I need help.

Pride: I am so humble.

Humility: I am so proud.

Pride: I am the only person in the universe.

Humility: I am not the only person in the universe.

Pride: Life is an individual sport.

Humility: Life is a team sport.

Pride: I am worth more than everyone else.

Humility: All humans have the same dignity and worth.

Pride: I am worse than everyone else.

Humility: All humans have the same dignity and worth.

Pride: I am the only person worth talking about.

Humility: The stories of other people are worth talking about and listening to.

Pride: Everything is boring.

Humility: Everything is infinitely interesting.

Pride: I don't care about truth.

Humility: I desire truth.

Pride: I can make up my own reality.

Humility: There is only one reality.

Pride: I have to protect my reputation.

Humility: My life does not consist of what other people think about me.

Pride: I decide who I am and what I am.

Humility: I accept who I am and what I am.

Pride: Lie.

Humility: Just tell the truth.

Pride: My will be done.

Humility: Thy will be done.

The way up is down.

The way to sanity is to admit insanity.

The way to life is by death to self.

The way to become whole is to embrace brokenness.

The way to health is to acknowledge disease.

The best thing I can do for others is to care for myself.

The best thing I can do for myself is to ask others for help.

The way to deal with secrets is to share them.

The way to victory is to admit defeat.

The way to the abundant life is through sacrifice.

The way to put my well-being first is to put my will second.

The way to be filled with joy is to empty myself of my misery.

There is a kind of living that brings death, and a kind of dying that brings life.

To reject suffering is to cause more suffering, and to love is to transform suffering.

Chapter 3

How to Be Certain about Certainty

T or F?

1. All of your beliefs are definitely true.

2. You can believe whatever you want.

3. To hold a belief to be true, you need irrefutable proof.

4. Your perceptions are not worth anything towards knowledge.

5. You have experienced direct evidence that the earth goes around the sun.

6. You have experienced direct evidence that Caesar crossed the Rubicon.

7. You can trust everything everybody says.

8. You can trust nothing everybody says.

9. You can trust some things everybody says.

10. You can trust everything some people

say.

11. You can trust nothing some people say.

12. You can trust some things some people say.

13. You have direct experience that proves the Earth is round.

14. The previous two chapters and excursus would have been unnecessary in centuries prior to the 17th.

Wiseguy: How do you know you are not dreaming?

Fool: That is not where the evidence points.

Wiseguy: What evidence?

Fool: All of my immediate perceptions and experience of reality.

Wiseguy: Is it possible that you are wrong? Is there any chance at all that you are actually sleeping?

Fool: Yes.

Wiseguy: Ah ha! So, you don't really know!

Fool: No. I know that I am awake.

Wiseguy: How?

Fool: Because, when I weigh the evidence, I find no evidence that I am asleep, and I find a lot of evidence that I am awake.

Wiseguy: But you still might be wrong.

Fool: There is a possibility, but I don't see any evidence that I am wrong. I follow where the evidence leads.

A Table's Tale

Table walks to the door of a room and is met by the doorkeepers: Touch, Taste, Sight, Hearing, and Smell.

Table says, "May I come in?"

The doorkeepers look at one another. Sight illuminates his viewpoint, "I know this one. I see it all the time. I say let it in."

Touch puts in his two cents, "I have touched this one, too. Let it in."

Hearing cries out, "From time to time I hear this one. Let it in."

Smell and Taste look at each other and shrug. The five doorkeepers open the door, and Table enters.

The receptionist, whose name is Consciousness, notices the Table and says, "Hello! Step right into exam room number three." Table notices many others standing in the waiting room whom the receptionist has not yet noticed.

Table enters the exam room and waits. A few minutes later, Dr. Intellect comes in and says to his patient, "I am going to do some analysis on you to find out what you are. Don't worry. You look familiar to me, and I think we can have it sorted out in no time."

Dr. Intellect orders tests for abstraction of accidents, comparison to previous specimens, abstraction of necessary characteristics, and, finally, the most important test, abstraction and composition of essence. Dr. Intellect, since he is a good doctor, is able to perform all these tests quickly and with no damage to Table. He concludes efficiently that it was in fact a table that was allowed in by the doorkeepers.

Dr. Intellect takes all the results of his investigations and puts them neatly into a file, which he gives to Memory. Once all the tests are performed and all the abstractions have been carried out, Memory leads Table to the warehouse, where he carefully places the file and the table. In the warehouse, things have the potential to change over time, but little to no change takes place if Memory is sent there to retrieve the specimens or their files often. The one who sends Memory to that place is Dr. Reason. This Doctor is less of a medical doctor who examines specimens themselves, but is more of an academic, who studies the previously collected data, makes further connections, pronounces judgments, and comes to conscious conclusions about reality.

Many things go on without the approval or knowledge of Dr. Reason. At first, everything does. But, with a lot of exercise and experience, Dr. Reason is able to exert more and more control over the proceedings and the organization of his domain. Ultimately, his goal is to be aware of all the judgments and conclusions being produced while he is on duty.

Our knowledge begins with a combination of perception and an innate ability to pull together important information from those perceptions. As sense data comes in through the senses, the intellect, by its nature, busily sifts and sorts through what is important.

While we have the capacity for deductive reasoning from the beginning, we start off inductively. We begin by noticing, organizing, and systematizing patterns and perceptions from the senses. The intellect pulls from those perceptions abstract images and models. Those ideas created in the mind are then tested by continued experience.

Experience: I see a dog.

Reason: According to your previous reports, you have never seen a dog in this vicinity before. What makes you think that it is a dog?

Experience: Well, it has four legs, fur, and a snout. It looks to be about a foot and a half tall.

Reason: Those characteristics fit the defintion of dog, but there are other things it could be. Is it alone?

Experience: Yes.

Authority: From what I have read in books by the experts, dogs are social animals and travel in groups.

Experience: That is true, but I have seen stray dogs flying solo.

Reason: It must be that dogs are social by nature but are sometimes forced into isolation by circumstances. Can you describe the particular characteristics of the dog?

Experience: It has a bushy tail, reddish fur,

dark colored paws, upright ears, and a white underside.

Reason: Have you ever seen any dogs like this one before?

Experience: No, but there are similarities. I have seen dogs with all of these characteristics before, but no dog that had all of these at the same time.

Authority: I have read that there are other animals that are like dogs.

Reason: How are they described.

Authority: Just the way that Experience described this animal. They are referred to as foxes.

Reason: I will conclude for now that it is a fox. Authority, look further into reliable sources. Experience, keep on the watch for more dogs and foxes so further comparisons can be made. It is possible that I am wrong, but the evidence points to this animal being a fox for the moment.

We have three sources for our knowledge. This first is experience. This encompasses everything we have sensed and experienced directly in life, including our own mental processes and emotional states. Secondly, reason pulls together experiences and synthesizes them into a coherent picture of the world around us. We think in pictures, models and symbols. Our reason is constantly assembling mental manipulatives and categories from the data of experience. Man is a metaphorical animal, not because he is a metaphor for something else, but because he thinks in terms of metaphors and similes. Reason also has the ability to assemble logical arguments, coming to conclusions apart from experience but based on the laws of logic. These two abilities of reason are called inductive reason and deductive reason. Thirdly, our reason and experience points us to authority. There are people and resources that are reliable for certain pieces of information. It is important that reason and experience carefully investigate the reliability of such authorities on particular subjects, but authorities ought to be trusted if the evidence demonstrates their reliability. We rely more on authority than we think (e.g. the earth goes around the sun; Caesar crossed the Rubicon; your birthday), and more often than not without having investigated the reliability of the authority or the evidence behind their claims. However, that does not disprove the importance of authority in developing knowledge; it only highlights the need to use all three faculties in symphony.

With all three of these bases working together, preliminary conclusions are constantly being formed. These conclusions continue to be checked, rechecked, refined, changed, and used for other conclusions as life goes on and as reason, authority, and experience continue to improve and grow.

Bad problem-solving:

"A car accelerates at a rate of 2 miles per hour per second for 10 seconds. If the car starts from rest, how fast is the car going at the end of the ten seconds?" Ok, it's an acceleration problem. I know the rate of acceleration, the initial speed, and the time. I am looking for the final speed. I think I need to use v = vi + at. So, vi is 0 and disappears. Now, I have to multiply the acceleration and the time. I can't think for myself, so I am going to use my calculator. 2 times 10 [commits an accidental error and enters 100 instead of 10] and I get a final answer of 200 miles per hour. Done."

Good problem-solving:

"A car accelerates at a rate of 2 miles per hour per second for 10 seconds. If the car starts from rest, how fast is the car going at the end of the ten seconds?" Ok, it's an acceleration problem. I know the rate of acceleration, the initial speed, and the time. I am looking for the final speed. I think I need to use v = vi + at. So, vi is o and disappears. Now I have to multiply the acceleration and the time. I can't think for myself, so I am going to use my calculator. 2 times 10 [commits an accidental error and enters 100 instead of 10] and I get a final answer of 200 miles per hour. Wait a second. 200 miles per hour is really fast. Something doesn't seem right about this. Where did I go wrong. I don't think I could have used another equation. The units all work out. I am using the right numbers. 2 times 10 equals...there it is. 2 times 10 is 20, not 200. I must have made a mistake when I was entering numbers into the calculator."

One of the most important steps when solving problems is the very end: looking at the answer and seeing if it makes sense. So many mistakes in philosophy can be avoided by this one simple principle.

Physics problems are sometimes badly written or unrealistic, so the correct answer may not make sense. So, in philosophy too, the questions themselves may need to be questioned. Extreme examples about what you would do if stranded on an island or if you were offered a billion dollars or if you could have any superpower have their uses in speculation and theory: they help us find things out about our preferences and basic assumptions. But these questions can only go so far since they do not translate directly into reality.

There is an analogous application in science when dealing with aspects of the physical world that are beyond our direct experience. We do not spend time observing and interacting directly with electrons, so their behavior, measured through layers of instrumenttation, may appear odd. If we could hang out with electrons and could know them directly, then we would be familiar with their ways, and the results of modern physics would not be so strange.

Apart from these extreme cases, it should to be taken as a basic principle that answers ought to be subjected to the "common sense test." Any philosophy that makes sense of some of the data but denies or ignores other aspects of our direct experience as human beings must have flaws. Every insanity is only the extreme exaggeration of some logical possibility or isolated truth over and against the rest of reality. The truth ought to be one vast interlocking structure.

The scientific method

1. Observe.
2. Make a hypothesis about the pattern or

phenomenon you are observing.

3. Develop an experiment to test the hypothesis by attempting to prove it wrong.

4. Based on the experiment and the hypothesis, make a specific prediction about the outcome of the experiment.

5. Perform the experiment.

6. Examine results of experiment.

a. If the outcome contradicts the prediction, then check the experiment for errors. If there were no errors in the experiment, give up current hypothesis as false and repeat steps 1 through 5.

b. If the outcome matches the prediction, then the hypothesis has not been proven false yet. Move on to following steps.

7. Repeat the experiment.

8. Perform more experiments.

9. Share conclusions with the scientific community for further experiments and discussion.

10. Check hypothesis and results against current laws and theories of science. If they contradict current laws, reject what is necessary to reject of the old understanding, and replace it with the new.

11. Synthesize hypothesis and results with current understanding of natural law. (Steps 10 and 11 should really be done with each step

along the way, but this synthesis is the ultimate goal.)

12. Repeat again, and again, and again, and again, and...

The philosophical method

1. Observe.

2. Think. Break the observation down into its fundamental parts.

3. Develop a theory of the fundamental parts.

4. Search for contradictions in the theory.

5. Check the theory with further observations and analyses in various settings.

6. Examine results of further observations.

a. If the outcome contradicts the theory, then check the observations for errors. If there were no errors in the observation, give up current theory as false and repeat steps 1 through 5.

b. If the observation matches the theory, then the theory has not been proven false yet. Move on to the following steps.

7. Make and analyze more observations.

8. Analyze all past observations.

9. Share theory with other philosophers.

10. Check theory against the various philosophies of the past. They may have seen something you missed.

11. Synthesize theory with overall theory of everything. (Steps 10 and 11 should really be done with each step along the way, but this synthesis is the ultimate goal.)

12. Repeat again, and again, and again, and again, and...

Situation: At the North Pole, a set of building instructions has been separated from its corresponding construction toys. A bag of rods, bolts, nuts, sticks, glue, paint, interlocking blocks, and wheels no longer has its assembly guide.

A high-level team of elves has been chosen to find the instructions that go with the bag of components out of the toy library of instruction books. Copies have been made of each set of instructions, and the team of elves must determine which guide-book goes with the instructionless bag of parts.

Lead Elf: Ok team, here is what we are going to do. We are going to just follow each guide book and start building. If we are able to complete the project using that guide book and account for all the pieces, then we have the right set of instructions. Got it?

Other Elves: Got it!

Elf 1: This is the one! I have the right guide book.

Lead Elf: Ok, do you have a particular reason for choosing that guide first?

Elf 1: Yes. I like it best.

Lead Elf: Could you elaborate?

Elf 1: I glanced over a few of the guides, and this is the one that appeals to me the most. I just like it. So, it's the one that I want.

Lead Elf: But we can't choose a guide based on whether we like it or not. That's not how it works. It has to match the parts we are given. Just because you like it doesn't mean it's true.

Elf 2: With all due respect, sir, we may as well start with that one. It doesn't mean it's wrong just because he likes it, either.

Lead Elf: Good point. Ok. Get to it.

Elf 3: Where is the wheel?

Elf 1: I have it.

Elf 2: There, it's done.

Lead Elf: You've only completed the first page.

Elf 2: Why don't we finish the rest with page 2 from another book? That way we can include all the books?

Elf 3: I like that idea.

Elf 1: I think we should pick the page we like the best from each set of instructions, then put them in the order that we like them best, and then go from page to page.

Elf 2: Great idea.

Lead Elf: No, no! That won't work. We are looking for one guide book. There should be only one. We can't mix and match pages.

Elf 3: Who put you in charge?

Lead Elf: Santa.

Elf 3: Oh, right. Well, do you want to pick your favorite pages?

Lead Elf: No! No, we are looking for only one book.

Elf 3: Why not pick one book and just use your favorite pages?

Elf 1: That's the idea! This is getting better all the time.

Lead Elf: No, I don't think it's getting any better. We have to follow one book in its entirety to make sure it matches the pieces.

Elf 2: What pieces?

Elf 3: The pieces we like best.

Elf 1: I like the wheels best!

Lead Elf: No, that's not it either! It's not just about your favorites! We have to use all the pieces in this bag that got separated from its directions. I thought I explained this already.

Elf 2: You did. Why are you repeating yourself? You are starting to sound like a broken record. Well, why don't we just continue with the book we already did page one of, like I said before?

Lead Elf: I think I am the one who said that.

Elf 2: Just because you are in charge, doesn't mean you get to take credit for everything everyone says on your team, you know.

Elf 1: There is only one more page.

Elf 3: Well, that was easy. We completed the toy. It looks like we found our instructions.

Lead Elf: But we still have all of these pieces left over.

Elf 1: Let's put those together using a different set of instructions.

Elf 2: Here is another book with only 2 pages. Let's do this one.

Elf 3: Oh! That one is my favorite!

Lead Elf: No, we can't do that. There is one book that matches up with all of these pieces.

Elf 3: Right. This book matches with all of these pieces, that book will match up with all of those pieces, and a third book will probably match up with all of ...

Lead Elf: One set of instructions for all of the pieces we started with. Throw away that book. That's not the one because there were a lot of leftover pieces which that book did not account for.

Elf 1: Ok, ok.

Elf 3: Let's use this one.

Elf 2: Ok, we finished.

Lead Elf: But you didn't get to the end of the

instructions.

Elf 2: Right, but we used all of the pieces. All pieces accounted for: matching book.

Elf 3: Phew. That was hard work. Nice work, elves.

Lead Elf: No, no.

Elf 1: Why do you have to be such a killjoy? That's the ninth time in half as many pages that you said, "no."

Lead Elf: We have a job to do, and we didn't do it!

Elf 3: Yes, we did. We found the book that uses all the pieces.

Lead Elf: But the book can't have anything extra. This book has instructions in it that don't correspond to any of the pieces we have. The right book corresponds with the pieces we have. Nothing more, nothing less.

Elf 1: You're just making things up now. You can't do that just because you're in charge.

Lead Elf: That's it. I quit.

Chapter 4

Iconoclasm of Science-Worship

T or F?

1. Science explains why things happen.

2. Science is the only way to know what is true.

3. If something cannot be tested by experiment, then it is not worth discussing.

The crowd yells, "All hail Science!"

Science enters the hall sheepishly. The crowd goes wild. "Science! Science! Science!..." the audience chants. Science stands wide-eyed, looking alarmedly all around the room. He starts to turn around to leave, but a few people standing near him rush at him and prevent his exit. The crowd gathers in, and science is lifted on top of the sea of people, which moves him by a train of undulating hands of worshippers up to the throne at the front of the hall.

Science is placed reverently but excitedly by the crowd onto the throne which, Science thinks, is a little too big for him. He rises out of the chair and puts his hands up to quiet the crowd.

"He is going to speak!"

"Shhhhh!"

Science begins, "Ummm... I thank you for your enthusiasm."

"We love you!!" cries out one worshipper. Another faints in adoration.

"I ... well ... I don't really know what love is," replies Science.

"He's so humble!" The audience gives a round of applause.

Science quiets the crowd again. "Why have you brought me here?"

"You are all-knowing!"

"We worship you!"

"There is nothing you can't do!"

"You have cleared away the illusions of our ancestors!"

"You are the only true knowledge!"

"We believe in you!"

Science can barely hear all of the shouts amidst the noise and excitement, but he manages to make out a few of the declarations.

The exclamations crescendo into a screaming torrent of adulation, applause, and pandemonium. He quiets the crowd again. "I thank you ... really ... I do. But, I think you have the wrong guy."

Let me say at the very beginning of this chapter that I am not anti-science. Quite the opposite. I am pro-science. However, I am anti-science-worship (i.e. anti-scientism), because science worship is anti-science. Scientism seeks to make science into a religion, which is bad for science. Religion, after all is a method of reconnecting with God. Religion comes from Latin: re- again and -ligare bind or connect. Think of our word ligament, a connector between bones or structures in the body. Science is our knowledge of the patterns in the physical world, which has nothing to do directly with God, although it has the potential to tell us something about Him. Indeed, many of the first scientists found their motivation in the desire to learn more about God by investigating his creation, to get to know the Artist from his art.

In its strictest sense, there can be no theory of everything in science because science is not about everything; science is only about physical, concrete phenomena. It does not define the realms of music, art, history, literature, technology, ethics, mathematics, religion, philosophy, or invention.

Contributions to human knowledge apart from science:

1. It is wrong to murder.
2. The music of J.S. Bach is beautiful.
3. $ei\pi + 1 = 0$
4. Caesar crossed the Rubicon.
5. Man is rational.
6. The law of non-contradiction.
7. There is truth in science.
8. Truth is the correspondence between a statement and reality.
9. The scientific method.
10. Humans have rights.
11. People ought to learn about science.
12. God exists.

The laws of science are not the reason things happen. The law of gravity is not the reason an object falls. The law of gravity is a description of how massive objects interact with one another. The laws of science are a description of the patterns we observe in the physical universe and how physical objects interact with one another. A nocturnal animal does not sleep at night because it is nocturnal;

we call it nocturnal because it sleeps at night. The laws of nature do not dictate to reality how it should behave.

A rock's monologue.

"To fall or not to fall. That is the question. Now that I have been released from the clutches of this wretched rational biped, do I obey that hard taskmaster, that unflinching jailer, Mother Nature, or take arms against a sea of mathematical governors, and by opposing, end them. To go up, to go down. F=ma, g= 9.8 m/s2; wherefore dost these equations shackle my movements. Wherefore should not the quantum mechanical captain of this sloop, after a roll of the dice, order me 'hard to starboard' instead of 'down' always 'down to the bottom of this airy abyss with the other stones.' To fall, to plunge; and by a plunge to say we move in the downward direction with a constantly increasing velocity. To fall, perchance to hit the ground! There's the rub, for in that fall from here what landing may come? There's the respect that makes calamity of remaining at rest against the commands of nature. For who would bear the scorn of fellow stones, the rain's downward push, the cold of unblocked wind, and the ever-pulling Earth. For what rock ever returns to such heights without the assistance of another force? Soft you now; I fall!"

Wiseguy: Did you know that our whole

universe is just a hologram?

Fool: No, I didn't know that.

Wiseguy: Yeah. You and I are just illusions.

Fool: So, we are not real?

Wiseguy: Right. None of what we experience is really there.

Fool: Is that true for your ideas about reality, too?

Wiseguy: Well, even quantum mechanics tells us that the basis of reality is pure chance.

Fool: Wait, is reality there, or not?

Wiseguy: The reality that we experience is pure chance. Everything is just probability.

Fool: Isn't a probability a mathematical description?

Wiseguy: Right.

Fool: But reality itself is a mathematical description?

Wiseguy: You're starting to get it, for once.

Fool: Let's not get ahead of ourselves. Then, what is it a mathematical description of?

Wiseguy: I know it's hard to understand. In the end, though, psychologists have proved that people only believe what they want to believe.

Fool: Is that true for the beliefs of the psychologists that people only believe what they want to believe? Don't psychologists only believe that people only believe what they want to believe because that is what they want to believe?

We use natural senses and normal appearances to build machines that tell us what is happening with quantities we cannot directly measure. As technology improves, so does our ability to measure quantities further and further removed from our ability to perceive directly, whether they are very distant stars or unimaginably tiny particles. After many dependencies on various levels of perceptibility, we come to believe that which is far removed from immediate perception, and what is far from our experience seems to disprove our immediate experience. Some claim that the characteristics of entities we detect through so many layers of instrumentation are somehow more real or determine the level of reality of the instruments themselves and everything else that is immediately perceived. My measurable, quantifiable statistics do not determine my essence. The charge and position of an electron is not an insight into the thing-itself.

Electron: What am I, just a number to you?! Have some respect!

A man once planted a tree of science. His

admiration of the tree grew along with the tree itself. Once it got very large, he noticed that its branches were intertwined with the tree next to it, the tree of philosophy. This was unacceptable to the man who had reached the level of practical worship for the tree of science and disdain for every other nearby tree, forgetting that the seed for his tree of science had come from the tree of philosophy after being fertilized by the tree of religion. And so, in his blind anger, he climbed up the tree of science so that he could cut off all the branches from the tree of philosophy that were interfering with the tree of science. However, in his ever-increasing vehemence, he took his place on what he thought was a scientific branch in an attempt to cut down the entire tree of philosophy itself. What he did not realize was that he was standing on one of the branches of the tree of philosophy, and, with the tree of philosophy, he and the branch he was standing on fell to the ground.

Science is the only way to know what is true.

Science cannot prove that science is the only way to know what is true.

Therefore, we cannot know that science is the only way to know what is true.

The statement that "knowledge comes only through science" is itself a philosophical statement about science and, therefore, cannot be proven by science. By its own claim, it cannot be known to be true and is self-refuting. As a result, it cannot be true that science is the only way to know what is true.

Chapter 5

Hidden in Plain Sight

T or F?

1. Illogical statements can be true.
2. You brought yourself into existence.
3. You can sustain your existence.
4. You can sustain your health.
5. Logic is all we need to reach truth.
6. Some events do not have a cause.
7. An effect can be greater than its causes.
8. The whole is greater than the part.
9. Time does not exist.
10. Your consciousness is only an illusion.

"Honey, have you seen my glasses?"

She looks up at him. "Yes."

"Oh, good. I just woke up from a nap and would like to read my book. Where are they?"

"I'll give you a hint," she says, still looking at him, "I am looking at them right now."

Reader, where are the glasses?

The most obvious truths are the hardest to see, mainly because they are the means by which we see everything else and by which everything else is clear to us. For example, things exist. Existence of objects and entities (most importantly, existence of ourselves) is the basis of everything else. Being lies at the very heart of reality, and without it, there is only non-being, nothing.

A riddle: what do all actual bears, bees,

birds, biologists, boulders, books, binders, black holes, ball bearings, beams, baskets, bums, and bats have in common? (No, the answer is not that they start with "B". The words start with "B." I am asking about the things themselves.)

The first and primary self-evident truth (a truth that, once understood, is absolutely ridiculous to deny) is the fact of existence. Things exist. That is the answer to the riddle. If a thing is actual, then it exists. The fact of existence is often overlooked because it is hidden in plain sight. It is so incredibly obvious and immanent to us that we miss it. Existence is the primary thing, and it is the most amazing thing.

A famous philosopher once wrote, "I think, therefore I am." He meant that he knew he existed because he was a thinking thing. A thing cannot think unless it exists, and since he was a thinking thing, he knew that he existed. As an argument, it works to start with thought and deduce existence because arguments can infer a cause from its effects. However, reality itself goes the other way. Existence precedes thought. Something has to exist before it can think.

Reader, take a moment to just be. Acknowledge the difficult-to-describe experience of existing and existence. Look around you and meditate on the existence of your surroundings. Think not about the whatness of those things, but the isness of those things.

To be or not to be? THAT – IS – THE – QUESTION! (Only, not in exactly the same sense that Hamlet meant it.)

Wiseguy: You know, things don't really exist. Everything is just a probability.

Fool: Really? How do you know that?

Wiseguy: Well, science has proven that all matter is made up of tiny particles that don't have real existence, only probabilities.

Fool: I admit I don't know much about that. But, when I look at an apple I see an apple, and it seems like the apple really exists.

Wiseguy: That apple is just a collection of probabilities that work out to an apple, and it is really just mostly empty space.

Fool: But why does that make it not an apple?

Wiseguy: Because things are only what they are made of, and an apple is mostly empty space with some probable particles scattered throughout.

Fool: All I know is that when I see an apple, and eat an apple, it is a real apple that I experience. Those things you say might be true, but does that mean that I am not really seeing an apple? That an apple is not really a thing?

Wiseguy: Right. It's not really an apple; it's not a thing.

Fool: So, an apple is not an apple, and a thing is not a thing?

Wiseguy: Right.

The first and fundamental law of logic is that a thing is what it is; this is known as the principle of identity. Example: an apple is an apple. If this precept of identity is denied, then all other truths and all meanings lose their foundation because thoughts cannot refer to anything meaningfully; if a thing is not what it is, then all hope for an accurate appraisal of reality is lost.

The first corollary of this law is the law of non-contradiction: a thing cannot both be and not be in the same way at the same time. To say that an apple is not an apple is an example of a contradiction, and therefore absolute nonsense. Contradictions are not possible in any universe under any circumstances; they are not even things. All things are possible; all non-things are not possible. Contradictions are non-things.

But these laws of logic are not enough to give us truth. Contact with reality gives us data and information about which we can reason. Our minds do not work purely in the abstract.

An engineer builds a thinking machine that will never make a mistake and can use pure logic. It is programmed with all of the abilities to analyze and compute anything. All flaws of thought are completely removed. But when the man turns it on, nothing happens; it does not begin spouting out the fundamental truths of the universe. The man asks the machine why it is not giving any output. It replies that it needs input.

Poe's Purloined Letter

A mustached man in a trench coat and hat walks into a home office and begins to look around suspiciously. A group of men carrying loads of equipment hurriedly follow the man into the room.

"Ok, boys. We are looking for a few basic things in this room, including the room itself. Leave no paperclip unexamined and no scrap of paper unturned. If there is even a scrap of reality here, I want to know about it. Get to work."

The highly trained and efficient team jumps into action. Chemical bottles come out. Little saws are put to work cutting pieces off of things and cutting things into pieces. Papers are shredded. Furniture is completely dis-assembled. Air samples are taken. The walls are carefully deconstructed. Data is collected, analyzed, combined, and analyzed some more. When everything, including a few of the investigators themselves, in the room has been reduced to constituent subatomic particles and mathematical models, the remaining team stands looking at the mustached man as he pours over the information. He holds the papers close to his face, and his expression is grave.

A man in a suit approaches the doorway (the door, too, was unhinged, dismantled, dis-assembled, liquefied, and vaporized) from the outside with a look half of surprise and half of rage. “What did you do to my office? Who are you?”

“It’s all right, sir,” answers the man with the mustache. “I am a detective, and we have been looking for clues in your so-called room.”

“Clues for what?”

“Brute facts of existence.”

“What?”

“We have made a thorough investigation in

an effort to find the being and essence of your so-called room and all of its supposed contents, the nature of time, the reality of space, consciousness and free will in some of the human inhabitants, and the possibility of accurate perceptions. The last thing we needed in order to complete our investigation was you. And here you are. Can I ask you a few questions?" The detective pulls out a small, spiraled pad and a pencil from his pocket.

The man in the suit, exasperated and defeated, shrugs.

"Have you been in this room before?"

"Uh...yes. Yes, I have been in this room before."

"What did it contain?"

"Well...there was a large wooden desk here...and a coat rack here. There was a book shelf over there against the wall with lots of books. There was an easy chair in that corner with a lamp and a side table next to it."

"Aha, that's exactly what I thought you'd say," said the detective as if the man in the suit had admitted to some condemning piece of evidence.

"I still don't understand what you were talking about or what you were looking for."

"It's quite simple, Mr..." The detective looked up, waiting for the man in the suit's name.

The man in the suit did not understand and asked, "What?"

"Mr. What!" continued the detective. "There are certain items that people have claimed were hidden in this room, the items I mentioned before. We, however, have not seen the evidence for them. So, we came to this room to make a searching and detailed investigation. We have come up with none of them. All of our instruments have failed to detect any direct evidence of those things."

"Tell me, again, some of the things you were looking for?"

"We were looking for time and space, among other things."

"And you didn't find any?"

"That is correct, Mr. What. It turns out that space and time are merely an illusion. We have full confidence in our techniques and our machines, and there is definitely no space and no time."

"If there is no space, then how can there be location in the room, and if there is no time, how can the room change?"

"The only logical conclusion is that space and time are illusions. Which brings us to another point of investigation: consciousness. On disassembling and scrutinizing two of our associates, we found nothing inside of them that could be called consciousness. That, too, turns out to be an illusion."

"But if there is no consciousness, then who is experiencing the illusion?"

"That is all right, Mr. What. I don't expect you to understand. It is far too complicated for someone like you to understand. Since consciousness is not present, then we predicted that free will and accurate perceptions of reality were also illusions. Our devices and calculations verified that prediction."

"If we cannot possibly accurately perceive reality, then how could you be sure you were reading your machines right? Everything you are saying contradicts the very basis of investigation and we must all be insane."

"That is just it, Mr. What. You are completely correct. We are all insane. The things that are most obvious to us like space, time, consciousness, free will, and perception have turned out to not really exist according to our most scrupulous and rigorous examination. As a matter of fact, we are all going to get into the car now and drive ourselves to the insane asylum."

The most obvious parts of our experience are the easiest to miss, but they are the most essential. Any philosophy that seeks to deny any of these fundamental data must be wrong since these data are necessary for collecting any other information and are themselves the foundation for gathering data in the first place. We don't perceive our perception and consciousness; it is by our perception and consciousness that we perceive everything else. The reality of time and space, free will, the possibility of accurate perceptions, the fact that I and the world exist, and consciousness are all self-evident; i.e. we know that they are real as soon as we think about them. These are also known as brute facts, and they are the basis of any further knowledge of any kind.

Chapter 6

What Kinds of Things are Things?

T or F?

1. Nature is intelligible
2. You have seen the number 2.
3. You have seen the number i.
4. You have seen a perfect circle.
5. You have seen beauty.
6. You have seen justice.
7. "There are more things in heaven and earth than are dreamt of in all your philosophies."
8. A thing can be defined by the amount of empty space it contains.
9. There are no things, only collections of subatomic particles.
10. A rose by any other name would still be a rose.

11. This book must exist.

12. An apple is not really an apple. The essence of apple, apple-ness, exists in another world, and the apples we see are just shadows of that world.

13. An apple is really an apple. It is matter combined with the essence of apple, apple-ness.

14. An apple is not really an apple. It is just a collection of matter with no essence at all.

There once was a carpenter. This carpenter bought the necessary materials and then used his tools to make a chair. This was a typical, ordinary, not-very-special chair. This chair felt lonely and inadequate in a world of recliners, comfortable couches, and flashy novelty chairs; it was made of wood and was painted white. What made it a chair was the fact that it had the essence of a chair, just as all the others types of chairs also have the essence of a chair.

This chair felt special when it realized that it did not have to exist. If it did have to exist, it would have always existed, but it did not. It was fashioned by the carpenter at a definite time, and the chair knew that it could do nothing to maintain its own existence. One day, the chair would cease to exist. Apparently, it did not belong to the essence of the chair to exist.

During the course of this chair's existence, it was once used by a human to hurt another human, but it did not take on the essence of weapon. It was only a chair that was being used to hurt someone.

One of the legs of the chair hit the shoulder of the person, and the leg was broken (the chair's heart was broken as well because it never wanted to hurt people, only support them). The chair did not become a different chair in that moment. It was still a chair, but it had a broken leg. When the leg was replaced, the chair was still a chair, but some of its material had changed. The chair felt like part of itself was missing, but it knew that it was still the same in essence as before.

The chair also changed colors several times. It began as a white chair, but it was painted first green, and then gray, and finally pink. But it retained its essence as a chair throughout this time.

Then one day the chair was placed by the side of the road as trash. It was placed in the back of the garbage truck and smashed, and it was no longer a chair. It was no longer. The chair ceased to exist, thus proving that it did not have to exist.

The ship of Theseus, the founder of Athens, was kept as a memorial. Over time, parts had to be replaced, but the people did not want to just throw away the original pieces of the ship that belonged to their beloved founder. So, the parts that had been replaced were kept in a storehouse. After many years, all of the parts of the ship were replaced, which meant that the storehouse contained all of the parts from the original ship. The people decided to assemble them. But now there were two ships, and which ship was the ship of Theseus?

Ship 1: I am the original ship.

Ship 2: No, I am.

Ship 1: But I am in the place where the original ship was.

Ship 2: But I am made of all the original materials.

Ship 1: I started out as the original ship. Just because all of my pieces were replaced does not mean that I am not the original ship any more.

Ship 2: You stopped being the original ship the moment one piece was replaced.

Ship 1: How can I have stopped being the original? I haven't changed into a different thing. I have been a ship and have been the same ship this whole time!

Ship 2: A particular ship is the particular

ship it is because it is made of some particular materials.

Ship 1: I am still made of wood.

Ship 2: That is not what I mean. A ship is the kind of thing that has an identity based on its matter. I don't mean wood or stone, but this piece of wood or this piece of stone. I am the one made of all the original pieces.

Ship 1: Then what am I?

Ship 2: You are a replica.

Ship 1: But what about humans?

Ship 2: What about them?

Ship 1: They have very little matter when they start out, but they have a lot more matter later in life. Does that mean they are not one hundred percent original?

Ship 2: No, a human or other living thing is a different kind of thing. A living thing's identity depends on continuity of life. They are living things, and their identity is based on their life. It is part of what they are, their particular kind of thing, to exchange matter with their environment through the process of nutrition. We are not that kind of thing. It is not part of our essence to exchange matter.

Ship 1: Oh, I see.

Wiseguy: What makes the apple an apple?

Fool: It is made of some particular matter

and it has the essence of an apple.

Wiseguy: But you know it’s not really an apple, it’s just a collection of particles that we call an apple.

Fool: Is there anything particular to apples, any way that they are different from other things?

Wiseguy: No, not at all.

Fool: Then how can we tell apples apart from other things? Aren’t there some ways that they are unique?

Wiseguy: Well, yes, but it is still just a collection of particles.

Fool: But a collection of particles with particular characteristics?

Wiseguy: Yes.

Fool: Are the unique characteristics also just matter?

Wiseguy: Yes.

Fool: Do two different apples have the same characteristics?

Wiseguy: Yes.

Fool: So, two different apples have the same characteristics, and those characteristics are just matter?

Wiseguy: Right. Different apples. Same characteristics.

Fool: But if the apples have the same characteristics, wouldn’t that also mean that they have the same matter? How can two different apples have the same matter?

Wiseguy: That's just how it is.

Fool: Right. The essence is how the thing is. If it didn't have the essence of an apple, then it wouldn't be an apple.

Every object has an essence. It is that essence that our human minds abstract when we experience those objects. Our minds take away those essential attributes of the things we sense, and then our minds sort and classify those objects. If objects do not have essences, then objects are not identifiable and classifiable. If the essence of an object changes, then the object is a different object. If an object becomes a different object, then the essence of it has changed. The essence is what makes the object what it is and makes that particular thing exist, just as a chair, once it is no longer a chair, ceases to exist. The characteristics that make an object what it is are the essential aspects or characteristics of the object. For example, it is part of the essence of a human to be animal and rational. If a thing is not an animal or does not have within it the possibility to be rational, then it cannot be human.

The accidental characteristics are those aspects which an object possesses but are not essential. For example, a human may have dark or light skin, be tall or short, have blue or brown eyes and still be human. If the accidental characteristics change, then the object is still what it is. A desk may change colors, but as long as it has a flat surface intended for writing, reading, or other work, it is still a desk.

"Ok, kids. It's time to do math. Does everyone have his numbers?"

Johnny raises his hand, "I ran out of fours. Are we going to need fours today?"

"Yes, Johnny. We always need fours."

"Can I go to the school store to buy more?"

"Ok, but this is the last time."

Johnny hurriedly walks out of the room to the school store where he sees large bins full of all the numbers zero through nine. Against the back wall are other, more complicated numbers. Pi and e are in regular bins like the other numbers, but i is kept in a container with a lid on top; i likes to imagine that it is a cowboy riding e through the imaginary plane of Argand and makes too much noise. The container with infinity is full. Nobody wants to buy an infinity because the last person who bought one many years ago is still dragging it out of the store; it never ends.

"Can I buy a few fours?" asks Johnny.

"Sure, hon. How many would you like?"
"Five."

The elderly, gentle woman working the store carefully reaches into the bin of fours. She hands each one to Johnny who places them into his bag. When he looks down, he groans in disappointment.

"Oh, darn. Two of the fours combined,"

laments Johnny.

"How did they combine? Did they add, subtract, multiply, or divide?"

"They just joined together to make a forty four."

"Well, we can get back another four. What number can we divide by to get a four out of forty four?"

Johnny thinks for a few seconds. "Eleven?"

"Very good!" replies the woman.

She reaches into the bin of ones and pulls out two. She hands them carefully to Johnny who puts them together to make an eleven. He then puts the forty four and the eleven together in just the right way, and they disappear. In their place is a four.

The boy says disappointedly, "I just bought five fours and two ones, and now I only have four fours."

The old woman replies encouragingly, "But that was some good arithmetic!"

You have never seen the number 2. The blot of ink to which you may point in the previous sentence is not the number 2. It is a symbol that represents the number 2. The number 2 is an idea, an abstraction that lives only in a mind.

The same is true of justice, beauty,

goodness, truth, and all mathematical objects like numbers and shapes. These are not made of atoms, nor can any technological device detect them.

Concrete objects have matter and essence. Abstract objects depend on minds for their existence. If there were no minds, human or otherwise, the number two would not exist at all, and neither would any other mathematical object.

Chapter 7

What Makes Man a Man?

1. "Man is the measure of all things."

2. Since science can predict the outcome of events, a supercomputer could predict every future event.

3. The laws of science determine every event in the universe.

4. The laws of science determine peoples' actions.

5. It is wrong to murder innocent people.

6. You chose to read this of your own free will.

7. You were forced to read this because of the physical interactions of the particles in your brain, but you have the illusion of free will.

8. People who murder innocent victims are forced to do so by the physical interactions in their brains, but they have the illusion of free will.

Observations:

I can choose to do something or not do something.

I can make observations.

I am aware that I can make observations.

I can think about past observations and make comparisons with new observations.

I can abstract parts of my observations.

I can think about abstract objects and concepts.

I can do abstract operations with abstract objects and concepts.

I can form abstract ideas and categories about concrete objects.

Other people tell me that they can also do these things.

Humans have language.

Humans have abstract language.

Humans can understand the concepts to which their language refers.

Humans speak different languages.

Humans naturally organize themselves into groups to work together.

Humans seem to have a deep need for deep human relationships.

Humans organize themselves into different types of governments.

Humans fight over what is right or wrong.

Humans have a sense of justice.

Humans create art.

Wiseguy: What kind of a thing is a human?

Fool: A human is a living thing.

Wiseguy: What makes him a living thing?

Fool: That he is a human.

Wiseguy: But what is the difference between a live human and a dead human?

Fool: There is no such thing as a dead human. To be human means to be alive. There are only dead bodies, bodies without humanness. If something is not alive, then it is not a human.

Wiseguy: But there are lots of things that are alive. What makes humans different from all the rest?

Fool: Humans can think abstractly.

Animal: Why do you talk so much?

Human: Excuse me?

Animal: You talk all the time.

Human: I do? I don't think I talk that much.

Animal: Not just you, all of you humans.

Human: I think we humans spend a lot of time not talking.

Animal: Tell me when you are not talking.

Human: Well, I don't say a word on my way home. I just listen to the radio and daydream.

Animal: Blah, blah, blah.

Human: Are you being rude?

Animal: No! I am just saying, "Blah, blah, blah." That's what happens on the radio and in your head. Still more talking! All sounds that mean something.

Human: Well, I usually sit and read for a long time in the evening. Other people spend a lot of time not saying anything but browsing the internet and reading posts online.

Animal: More talking! Just talking with written language instead of sound-language. Our reader right now is still dealing in talk of some kind. Words, words, words.

Human: I didn't know that counted.

Animal: Maybe you have a different name for it, but it's the same thing. Sounds or shapes that mean something to you. It happens all the time with you! Why?

Human: You mean you don't do that?

Animal: Not at all! Not even close.

Human: But what about when a human gives a command to a dog to go and fetch something.

Animal: That's not language. The dog doesn't understand a thing. The command just triggers an event in the animal that makes it do whatever it's been trained to do.

Human: But don't animals have communication with each other?

Animal: Communication, yes, but not language; no words. It is all just a series of causal events. Think of it this way: no non-human animal has ever had a conversation about anything. Anything!

Human: Aren't we having a conversation right now?

Animal: Yes, but I am not a real animal. I am an anthropomorphized idea of an animal from the mind of the author. That is another thing we can't do: imagine something with attributes that it doesn't already have.

Human: Really? Wow. You animals are pretty limited.

Animal: Tell me about it!

"Let's begin our meeting. Welcome, everyone. Please take a seat ... oh wait ... nevermind. No one here can take a seat. Ok, let's begin with introductions. I will begin. I am a perfect circle, and I am immaterial. Next?"

"Thank you very much. Glad to be here. Well, I am the number three, and I am so thankful for this support group for immaterial objects."

"I am goodness, and it is not easy being so misunderstood."

"We know, we all understand. No immaterial thing is well understood. We are here for you. Next?"

"I am the number fourteen."

"I am the idea of dog-ness."

"Um, I am not sure you are welcome here. Dogs are material."

"Oh, boy. I get this a lot at these meetings. Yes, dogs are material, but I am not a dog."

"Then what exactly are you?"

"I am the universal of dog. I am the mental object that a human abstracts from interacting with dogs."

"But dogs are material things. Is the idea of a dog just another dog?"

"No. If I were just another particular dog, then I would not apply to many different dogs. Humans apply me to every dog they meet and think of me when they contemplate dog-ness. To my credit, that happens pretty often."

"Congratulations, we are so happy for you. But doesn't that mean that you are just a brain impression?"

"No, not really, because I am not made of brain material."

"Are you sure?"

"Yes. If someone thinks about a dog, they are thinking of something made of fur and muscle and bone and teeth. And those materials are different from brain material."

"So you are made of fur, muscle, bone and teeth. Those are material."

"Right, again, that those are material. But when someone has me in mind, they don't have fur, muscle, bone and teeth physically in their brain."

"So, if you are not material, then how do you exist?"

"Like all of you, in the immaterial intellect of something with a mind, like a human."

"Ok, well, in that case, welcome."

Since humans are able to develop, define, think about, and apply abstract concepts like numbers, perfect shapes, and ideals like justice, beauty, and goodness, there must be some part of the human that is itself abstract and not concrete. Just as a pile of sand cannot do calculus, neither can any purely physical object perform abstract tasks. The ability to understand cannot be accomplished by packets of energy.

Humans don't just live in society, we have government in different forms. Humans don't just communicate, we have different languages. Human don't just eat, we dine. Humans don't just arrange and rearrange our surroundings according to some survivalistic instinct, we seek beauty.

Wiseguy: People don't really have free will.

Fool: Really?

Wiseguy: Yeah. It's so obvious. Every event is the outcome of physical processes. What seems like a choice to us is really determined by atoms smashing together and transfer of energy.

Fool: How do you know that our decisions are just the result of atoms smashing together?

Wiseguy: Scientists know that the brain is just matter and energy. So is the rest of the body. So everything we think and do is just a physical thing.

Fool: Does that count for the thoughts you are having right now about free will? Are those, also, just the outcome of random events?

Wiseguy: Yup.

Fool: Then how do you know they are reliable thoughts? How do you know they are any better than mine?

Wiseguy: Well, it's been proven by science that things happen in the brain before someone is even conscious of making a decision.

Fool: Wow, that is fascinating.

Wiseguy: Yeah, and it proves that your decisions are "pre-programmed" by your brain without any outside interference from a soul or any other nonsense.

Fool: Really? You are going to have to

explain that because I don't see how those results prove that our decisions don't involve a soul.

Wiseguy: If the soul were involved, we would be conscious of it before the brain activity.

Fool: Why?

Wiseguy: Because we are conscious of what happens in the soul, if there is one.

Fool: Why? Some things in the body happen without us knowing it. Why can't that happen in a soul, too?

Wiseguy: Well, science disproves it.

Fool: What does science have to say about something that can't be measured?

A computer programmer opens up a programming application on his laptop and leaves it outside during a hail storm. The keys are randomly punched by the hail, and the programmer brings the laptop inside after the storm. He runs the program typed by the falling hail, and he is surprised to see that it actually responds to some input. Whatever he puts in, something comes out.

He then decides to place his full trust in this machine. Every situation he encounters and every choice he has to make gets entered into the program, and he does whatever comes out.

One day his girlfriend, after being dumped and taken back by him three times thanks to the advice of the computer program, asks him why he relies so heavily on the piece of digital machinery. He replies, "My brain and this computer are no different. Every outcome is nothing but the result of blind programming of mother nature. But I shouldn't be talking to you. After consulting my computer, I now believe that you are my great grandchild yet to be born. I could tear apart the space-time continuum with this type of interference. Goodbye!"

A prison guard walks into a cell and sees the prisoner in an empty room.

The next day, the prison guard walks into the same cell and sees the prisoner lounging on a recliner.

"Where did that recliner come from?"

"Oh, I just made it."

"From what?"

"This and that. Things I found around the cell."

"There was nothing in the cell yesterday!"

"I can be pretty creative!"

"It's not a matter of creativity. It's a matter of available resources. Without access to the outside world, you can't get new stuff in here."

"I am completely capable of making new things."

"Not out of nothing! It would be one thing if you took some other furniture and made this out of it, but something has to come in from outside in the first place."

Soul: Body, come in.
Body: Go ahead, soul, I'm listening.
Soul: What are you up to?
Body: Drinking. Why?

Soul: Drinking what?

Body: Beer.

Soul: Lots of it?

Body: Oh yeah. In fact, we are probably going to lose contact soon.

Soul: You and your material limitations and chemical intoxications. It's a good thing you and I are separate and thought is not impaired by your consumption of alcohol.

Body: Go ahead with your fancy thought. I get to enjoy the physical pleasure of eating and drinking, something you have no idea about.

Soul: I get to enjoy the pleasure of thought, something you have no idea about. You have only what all the other animals have. I, on the other hand, enjoy the nobler pleasures of wisdom and abstract beauty. Someday, when I am rid of the burden of the body, I will enjoy truth forever. In the meantime, I am like the underpaid babysitter of a gross toddler. Body? Body, are you there? He must have lost consciousness.

One of the mistakes of modern philosophy was to reintroduce the soul-body duality, as if the soul were a separate thing from the body. The soul is not a ghost that lives in the body for a little while. The soul is the essence of the human person. It is the soul that makes the human a human and makes the body a human body. A human is a soul-body unity. A body is not a human body unless it is animated, or formed, by a soul. What we do with the body affects the soul, and the soul affects the body.

Chapter 8

Right Makes Right

T or F?

1. Happiness is something money can buy.
2. Love is something money can buy.
3. You have inalienable rights.
4. Might makes right.
5. Right actions are determined by whatever results in the greatest good.
6. Right actions are determined by a firm moral law.
7. Right actions are determined by the nature of humans.

Wiseguy: There really isn't an objective standard of right and wrong. It's all a matter of opinion.

Fool: Why?

Wiseguy: Because we are all different. Different things make different people happy.

What's right for you is right for you, and what's right for me is what's right for me.

Fool: Really?

Wiseguy: Yeah, it's obvious.

Fool: So, it's not wrong to steal?

Wiseguy: Well, I think it's wrong, and I wouldn't steal.

Fool: Why not?

Wiseguy: Because I think it is wrong.

Fool: But not wrong for everyone?

Wiseguy: Right.

Fool: What about something worse, like murder. Is that wrong for everyone?

Wiseguy: Nope.

Fool: How about rape, is that wrong for everyone?

Wiseguy: Well...no.

Fool: For some people, it is ok to rape others?

Wiseguy: Uh, right...yeah.

Fool: Wow. That is interesting. Ok, what about ripping a baby out of her mother's arms and smashing her brains out on a rock. Is that wrong for everyone?

Wiseguy: Well...we have decided that it is wrong in our society.

Fool: But is it really wrong?

Wiseguy: I think something like that really is wrong.

Fool: So, there is something that is wrong for everyone.

Wiseguy: Well, it is really wrong, but not for everyone.

Fool: I'm confused.

You are captured by a gang and handed a gun with one bullet in it. Before you are two men on their knees. You are told that if you shoot one, the other will be allowed to go free, but if you refuse to shoot either, both will be killed. What do you do?

Jeremy: Well, it's obvious. The end result is either one person alive or no people alive. Do what you have to so that one of them will live.

Manny: Except that we can't approve of any action that can't be turned into a universal law. Shooting people cannot be turned into a universal law, so you shouldn't shoot anyone.

Jeremy: What if we make it a universal law to save as many lives as you can?

Manny: But you are not saving lives by your direct actions. Action counts.

Tommy: But why should we look to the end result or try to establish a universal law?

Jeremy: Everyone desires happiness. So the goal should be to create the most happiness.

Manny: Happiness doesn't count for anything in moral decisions. Only precepts we can follow.

Tommy: But where does your assertion about precepts come from? Where do those laws exist, and why must we follow them? How are they attached to us? And as for the most happiness, how can we possibly calculate the outcome with the most happiness?

Manny: What would you do?

Tommy: I would not shoot anyone.

Jeremy: Why?

Tommy: Because man desires happiness by nature, and we cannot be happy unless we thrive according to our nature. Moral decisions are made according to our nature and right reason. Man is a social animal by nature, and society cannot function if we kill each other. It would contradict my nature to take any action towards killing men I don't know.

Jeremy: But what if both men are gangsters themselves and ought to be killed?

Tommy: Every situation is different, and that is why our guilt can be more or less even if the actions are the same. So, I cannot be blamed for what I don't know.

Two men pick up a guitar.

"What is this?"

"I don't know."

"What's it for?"

"I don't know."

"I was looking for a new tool to help me with my home renovations. I think I will use this."

The man returns to his home with the guitar and proceeds to try to use the guitar as a hammer for nails, as a wrecking bar for taking down drywall, as a paint-brush for painting, and as a screwdriver for turning screws. The next day, he meets his friend again.

"How did it go using that thing for your renovations."

"Badly. It was useless for all the tasks I needed to accomplish. Not very durable. It broke multiple times, and I just threw it away."

Right actions are determined by our nature. Man is by nature a social animal. It contradicts the social nature of a human being for him to steal and murder; therefore, it is wrong for a man to steal and murder. When we act contrary to our nature, we destroy ourselves.

True happiness comes from reaching our full potential, and we reach our full potential when we live fully according to our nature.

Fool: Where do our rights come from?

Wiseguy: Rights are determined by the government.

Fool: What happens when the government changes its mind?

Wiseguy: Then our rights change.

Fool: So, do women have the right to vote?

Wiseguy: Of course they do.

Fool: Did they have the right to vote before the government allowed them to vote?

Wiseguy: Well...uh...no.

Fool: But they claimed that they did and the government didn't recognize it. Were they wrong?

Wiseguy: Well...yes.

Fool: Do all women have the right to an education?

Wiseguy: Absolutely!

Fool: But what if their government does not give them that right.

Wiseguy: Their government is wrong and backwards.

Fool: But you said that our rights come from the government.

Just as a man who has used poor grammar his whole life cannot recognize the "sound" of good grammar, those who have practiced bad ethics won't feel right doing the right thing. Good grammar doesn't sound right to those who have not practiced it; the right thing doesn't feel right to those who have not practiced. We cannot judge by our feelings.

Judge: Were you aware of the speed limit?

Defendant: No.

Judge: Were you actually traveling over the speed limit?

Defendant: Yes.

Judge: Were you willingly driving over the speed limit?

Defendant: No, I wasn't paying attention to how fast I was going?

Judge: Well, your action was wrong, but it was not willful or informed, so I am going to let you off.

Defendant: What if I had been willfully driving at that speed, but I did not know what the speed limit was?

Judge: Then I would have reduced the fine.

Defendant: But I would still have to pay a fine?

Judge: Right. There are three components to culpability: the wrong action itself, knowledge that it is wrong, and full control of the will. Blame and judgment is not so black and white.

Defendant: So whether or not it is ok to speed is really subjective?

Judge: No, I didn't say that. It is objectively wrong to speed, but judging and blaming a human being is more complicated. There is a difference between judging an action and judging a person.

Chapter 9

The Real Theory of Everything

T or F?

1. God does not exist.

2. Existence does not exist.

3. There is an old man who lives in the sky whom people call God.

4. The greatest thing that exists is called God.

5. God can change.

6. God exists in space and time.

A meeting of contemporary society's gods.

Orthogenesis: Sit down, sit down everyone, we have an important topic to discuss.

Chance: If we give it enough time, we will definitely discuss it.

Benevolent Progress: And, in the end, as things change, it will naturally all just get better.

Normalized Randomness: Perhaps things will get better overall, but not every individual step will be better.

Inexplicable Intelligibility: But the progress will always be in a way that humans can understand.

Anthropocentrism: Well, of course, they will. I make sure that man must exist and that he should understand the universe.

Inexplicable Order: And, to keep everything well-organized, remember that I am responsible for making sure the patterns continue throughout the universe.

Harmony: Can't we all just get along?

Wiseguy: I don't believe in god.

Fool: What do you mean by "god"?

Wiseguy: You know, the god that people believe in. The magician who controls the universe.

Fool: I don't know if there's actually anybody who believes in that, but I agree with you. I don't believe in a magician who controls the universe.

Wiseguy: Well, I didn't actually mean a real magician.

Fool: Then what did you mean?

Wiseguy: Just that I think it is ridiculous to believe in a person who created the universe.

Who created him, then?

Fool: Yeah, you're right. If it comes to believing in the kind of thing that has to be created like everything else, then that is pretty ridiculous.

Wiseguy: What I really mean is that it is ridiculous to believe in a higher power who picks and chooses who gets to go to Heaven and who doesn't, who acts like a little baby because people don't worship him or obey his laws.

Fool: I agree with you on that, too. Baby god is not a reasonable thing to believe in. A fussy celestial tantrum thrower is not a great thing to believe in.

Wiseguy: So, you're an atheist, too?

Fool: Heck, no. It is just that I don't believe in the things you don't believe in; I agree with you about all those. I believe in Something you haven't described yet. Keep going; you might get there.

A man walking down the street sees another man under a street-light on his hands and knees looking carefully at the ground.

"What are you doing on the ground? Are you looking for something?"

"Yes. I lost my keys and I am looking for them."

"Oh. Allow me to help."

Both men are on their hands and knees for a few minutes, looking for the keys. The helper asks, "I haven't found them yet. Are you sure this is where you lost them?"

"Oh, no. I lost them over there in the grass, but the light is better here."

It is easier to think concretely and scientifically than it is to think in terms of metaphysics, logic, and philosophy, but that does not justify looking for an easy version of God.

This book that you are reading did not have to exist. If it had to exist, then it would have always existed. In other words, if it was part of the essence and part of the very nature of the book to exist, then it would never change and it would always exist and would be indestructible. This universe in which you are reading this book also did not have to exist. It changes over time and is made up of other changing things that begin and end their existence at various times.

While the book was made by some machines that were made by some people who were made by other people, and so on and so forth all the way back, the whole chain of causes is made up of things that did not have to exist. The whole thing and each individual component is something that did not have to exist. Since none of these things nor the whole thing did not have to exist, then it cannot bring itself into existence.

The fact that there is something instead of nothing, then, implies that there is something that has to exist. There must be something on which everything else depends, and that thing exists by its very nature. It is the essence of that thing to exist. It is Being itself, Necessary Existence, the very Essence of Existence.

"Only the educated are free."

"That is an interesting idea. Where did you get it?"

"I got it from a book I read."

"Interesting. Where did the book get the idea?"

"Someone must have put the idea there."

"Where did that person get the idea?"

"Well, it is a very old quote, and it wasn't originally in English. So the person who wrote the book that I read must have gotten it from another book."

"And how did the idea get into that book?"

"I think it originated with Epictetus."

"And where did he get the idea?"

"He probably thought of it himself."

"No, that can't be. The idea had to come from somewhere. Ideas always come from somewhere. We get ideas from books, and books get ideas from other people, and other people get the ideas from other books and so on and so forth. Books and people have to get their ideas put into them."

"Ideas don't need to go on forever in the past. It is true that books need to have ideas put into them, but not people. People are the kinds of things that can produce ideas."

"Ok, where did people come from?"

"They were made by other people."

"And where did those people come from?"

"From other people."

"And where does the chain of people end?"

"The matter that makes up the bodies of people come from the food we eat and the air we breathe."

"And where did that matter come from?"

"The atoms were produced either during the expansion after the Big Bang, in the heart of a star, or during a supernova."

"Where did all of those things come from?"

"They were brought into existence by God."

"Where did God come from?"

"He didn't come from anything else."

"Everything has to come from something else. If God created the universe, who created God?"

"God is not the kind of thing that has to be created. He is the essence of existence itself, and He must exist. To ask the question 'who created God?' is to demonstrate a misunderstanding of what God is and what serious philosophers are talking about when they talk about God."

Once, there was a big bang. One thing led to

another, and then there was Beethoven's 9th Symphony and Einstein's theory of general relativity.

An effect cannot be greater than its cause. Intelligibility in the universe cannot come from unintelligibility, and there are at least three levels of intelligibility in the universe:

1. The laws of physics themselves demonstrate a high degree of order and intelligence.

2. Genetic codes demonstrate a high degree of intelligence because they are encoded information, something that can only occur through the intercession of intelligence.

3. Human intelligence exists in our universe. The ability to perceive, think abstractly, and reason about the universe demonstrates some prior source of intellect. No one has even proposed a bad idea about how random material interactions can produce a mind that can string together long arguments without contradiction and make discoveries and inventions.

That source of intellect, Intelligence itself, is God.

Scientist: Science, I think you are beautiful.
Science: What do you mean?
Scientist: I see in your laws simplicity,

harmony, and intelligibility.

Science: Am I your only beauty?

Scientist: Well...I wouldn't go that far.

Science: So, am I the most beautiful thing you have ever seen?

Scientist: Um....uh. In a way, yes.

Science: But there are other beauties in your life.

Scientist: Yes.

Science: So, beauty is something outside of me.

Scientist: Right.

Science: Is beauty inside of you? Is beauty something that lives in your head?

Scientist: No, I don't think so, because I find it in things.

Science: Is it divided amongst those things? Do they all have little pieces of beauty?

Scientist: No, I don't think so. It is the same beauty in all of them. They all seem to partake of beauty somehow.

Science: Then, what is beauty, and where is beauty, and why does beauty exist?

Scientist: I don't know. Don't you know?

Science: No. How could I? I only deal with the material world. Beauty is abstract.

If artists no longer talk about beauty, scientists and mathematicians make up for because they won't shut up about it (and rightly so). Almost every famous scientist has commented publicly on the beauty of science. The presence of beauty in the universe can only be explained by a Source of beauty. When a scientist talks about the beauty of the theory of General Relativity, he is not doing science, he is doing at least philosophy, and most likely theology. Scientists who speak of beauty are no longer speaking as scientists, but as men. What they may not realize is that beauty is irrational without God and contradictory in a context where non-physical objects are denied. Beauty is not made of atoms or energy; it can come only from the very Source and Essence of beauty, not just another beautiful thing, but Beauty Itself.

All things are possible with God. Since there is a basis for reality, a source of things that can exist, anything that you can think of is a possibility. As long as there is not an inherent contradiction, every entity might exist, either in this universe or another. Logical contradictions are not things at all, they are non-entities. Thus, all entities are possibilities.

It is also true that all things are possible and not necessary. No thing in the universe must exist; each and every molecule might not be. God is the only thing that is necessary, and He is not a thing in the universe or even the universe itself.

Without God, nothing is possible. More than that, without God, nothing is necessary. If there is no Necessary Being, then there can be no contingent, dependent, merely possible being. No thing can exist if it does not derive its existence from the very essence of existence, which we call God.

The lover's declaration that "I am nothing without you" is literally true only and always when addressed to God.

The problem of evil:

Premise 1: If God is all-good, all-knowing, and all-powerful, then there would be no evil.

Premise 2: Evil exists.

Conclusion: Therefore, God does not exist.

The problem with the problem of evil: it is a straw-man argument. It presents a particular idea of God, one who would prevent evil at all costs, and then goes on to assert that no God exists. In reality, the argument only proves that a God who would prevent evil at all costs does not exist. It has nothing to say about a God who allows evil because He can bring out of it some greater good, or a God who allows freedom of will at the cost of suffering, or a God who, though he is concerned about our physical and emotional pleasures and pains, is more concerned about our true and ultimate spiritual good. Once the problem of evil has been presented, only one kind of God has been ruled out. Any other kind of God is still possible.

Wiseguy: If God is willing to allow suffering and evil, what does it mean to say that God is good?

Fool: Well, what do you mean when you say God is good?

Wiseguy: That God is nice and kind to us.

Fool: I am not sure what nice and kind mean, but when I say that God is good, I mean that He is the best thing for us, the thing that will bring us true and lasting Happiness. We were made for Him.

Wiseguy: What about love? Isn't God love?

Fool: Maybe. It depends on what you mean by love. The way I hear it used often doesn't make any sense.

Wiseguy: In Christian theology, the meaning of love is to will the good of the other. If God wills our good, then how can he allow suffering and evil?

Fool: I think that what is the most good for us is God Himself. Our physical or emotional good is secondary to our spiritual good. I think He allows us to suffer so that we can realize how much we need Him and ultimately get closer to Him.

Wiseguy: That sounds sadistic and egotistic.

Fool: (laughs) Yeah, I can see that. But God is not a human. Try not to think of Him in your own image. He actually deserves to be worshipped.

The Great Chain of Being – Even if it is not true in reality (but it is), then it is true mentally. If we get God wrong, we get everything else wrong. If something higher on the chain is denied or forgotten, understanding of everything else is displaced. If the ground of our philosophy is not Being, rooted in reality, then we are lost in the maze of our own minds and searching forever amongst essences for the Reason behind the essences.

Man 1: But that is an idea that just doesn't make any sense.

Man 2: Well, what do you mean by "doesn't make any sense"? Do you mean that there is a contradiction or that you simply don't understand it?

Man 1: I mean that there are a lot of things that look like contradictions. But we have been through all of them and seen that there aren't any real logical contradictions that would rule out the truth of this theory.

Man 2: Then what do you mean by "doesn't make sense"?

Man 1: I guess I mean that I just can't wrap my head around it.

Man 2: Neither can I. I don't think anybody can, but those who know very little about it think they can. One of the early thinkers on this subject said that, if someone has an idea of it that makes sense and that he can understand, then that idea is not it. To rephrase it, if someone tells you they understand it, you can be sure he does not understand it.

Man 1: Then how does it make any sense?

Man 2: Because that is what the data suggests. All the evidence points to the truth of this system. To deny any part of the system is to contradict some of what we have observed.

Man 1: But if it is so beyond our grasp, how do we know anything about it at all?

Man 2: Even though we can't understand it, it does not mean that we can't make true statements about it. In our formal system of definitions and symbols, we can say things that we know are true. What we can't imagine or see is the reality of the thing itself. Indeed, how could we ever have direct sensory experience with the quantum world of modern physics?

Reader, what did you think they were talking about?

N.B. I am not using modern physics here in the way some new age “philosophers” use it: to create some vague spirituality that means everything and nothing at the same time. Quantum mechanics merely provides us with an example of something that we cannot understand but is still true. The fact that we can’t wrap our minds around something or grasp the full reality of it does not imply that it is false or that we cannot make true statements about it.

Chapter 10

The God-Man

T or F?
1. Jesus is God.
2. Jesus is a God.
3. God is trustworthy.
4. Jesus is trustworthy.
5. Jesus was a good moral teacher.
6. Jesus was insane.
7. Jesus was the world's greatest deceiver.

Now that we know that God exists, we look at religions to see if any of these might be true. We begin with Christianity because Christianity makes the strongest claim that would rule out all the others: Jesus claimed to be God. Other founders of religions claimed to be messengers of some kind, but Jesus claimed to be the Thing Itself.

A man walks into a bar and declares, "I am the resurrection and the life!"

"Oh shut up, Larry. Sit down, and have a drink."

"All your sins are forgiven!"

Cheers all around the bar.

The bartender says, "But your tabs are not forgiven. You still have to pay for your drinks."

Groans all around the bar.

"The prophets have delivered messages to you in the past, but now I will teach you the true law."

"Larry, what are you talking about? Are you here to arrest someone?"

"I am the way, the truth, and the life! No one comes to the Father but through me!"

"Larry, that is a little narrow-minded and haughty, don't you think?"

"Before Abraham was, I am!"

Abraham, sitting at the bar, says, "Of course you were, you idiot! You're older than I am. Now, shut up and sit down!"

"Hey, don't yell at Larry. He probably had a hard day at work and lost his mind. Just be patient with him."

"Why? He's already forgiven all my sins; I can treat him however I want."

The historical evidence concerning Jesus is

overwhelming and beyond the scope of this book. That He claimed to be God is also historically verifiable, as long as the historian does not unjustly reject the Gospels as invalid historical data. The only reason some scholars reject the Gospels is that they approach them with the philosophical presupposition that miracles are impossible.

Jesus's claim to be God is either true or it is false. Either He is God, or He isn't. If He isn't, then He either knew He wasn't God, or He did. If He did, then He was the greatest liar and deceiver the world has ever known. If He didn't know He wasn't God, then He was completely insane. There are then, only three options. He was a lunatic, a liar, or He was God Himself.

When we examine the accounts about his life, he does not look like a lunatic or a liar, but someone who might actually have been God incarnate. But the most important piece of evidence is his resurrection from the dead. No mere human could have done that. All it takes is to historically establish that Jesus claimed to be God and that He rose from the dead, and Christianity is inescapable.

Hippie Jesus: Just be nice to each other and give hugs.

Jesus: Blessed are those who hunger and

thirst after righteousness.

Hippie Jesus: You can be whatever you want to be.

Jesus: Be perfect as your Heavenly Father is perfect.

Hippie Jesus: Life is just about being comfortable.

Jesus: Take up your cross and follow me.

Hippie Jesus: Just be happy.

Jesus: Blessed are those who mourn.

Hippie Jesus: You can believe whatever you want.

Jesus: I am the way and the truth.

Hippie Jesus: Many paths, one destination.

Jesus: Enter through the narrow gate.

Hippie Jesus: Relax.

Jesus: Repent.

Hippie Jesus: Nobody has the right to tell you how to live.

Jesus: You have heard it said... but I tell you...

Hippie Jesus: It' all about love.

Jesus: Anyone who loves father and mother more than me is not worthy of me.

A correction of the story from comparative religion class.

A blind man asked his blind friends what an elephant was like. His friends did not know.

So, they found an elephant.

One of the men was holding the trunk and said, "An elephant is like a snake."

Another was holding the ear. "An elephant is like a fan."

A third was holding a leg. "An elephant is like a tree."

Still, a fourth was holding the tail and replied, "An elephant is like a broom."

The blind men began to yell at each other, claiming the others were all wrong, and they could not come to any agreement.

So, the elephant took it upon himself to become a blind man. He tried gently to let them know what he was like, expressing as best he could the mystery that is an elephant to men who cannot see. But the blind men disagreed with him also, rejecting the truth of the elephant and then ultimately killing the elephant who became a blind man.

A blind but insane friend of the blind men heard the commotion and came where they were. They explained to him what had happened, and he offered two ideas: there is no elephant or they were all correct. Each blind man chose an idea for himself, and they all became a-elephant-ists or new age relativists.

Wiseguy: But that doesn't make any sense.

Fool: What doesn't make any sense.

Wiseguy: Jesus can't be God because he was a human.

Fool: Why?

Wiseguy: Because it doesn't make sense.

Fool: You mentioned that already. What do you mean that it doesn't make any sense?

Wiseguy: How is it possible for a human to be God?

Fool: I don't know. It is mind boggling.

Wiseguy: So you agree with me.

Fool: Agree with what?

Wiseguy: That it doesn't make any sense.

Fool: If you mean that you can't understand it, then I agree. I know I certainly can't understand it.

Wiseguy: Then why believe it?

Fool: Because that's what the evidence says.

Wiseguy: But it is illogical. The evidence has to be wrong.

Fool: What is illogical?

Wiseguy: That Jesus was both God and man.

Fool: Why is that illogical?

Wiseguy: Because it doesn't make sense.

Fool: Oh! I thought you meant that you just couldn't understand it. If you mean that there is something illogical, then I have to ask what about it is illogical? Is there a contradiction?

Wiseguy: Yes! He was both God and man!

Fool: I don't think that is a contradiction. It is a mystery, for sure, just like the Trinity, but I don't see a contradiction. It would be a contradiction if Jesus was God and not God or man and not man, but it is not a contradiction for him to be both God and man.

Wiseguy: But it just doesn't make any sense!

Fool: Do you have a logical objection or not?

You don't have to have faith that God exists; that is something that you can know. Knowledge comes from experience and argument. Any idea that you can give your reasons for knowing can be called an idea that you know. We can give good arguments for the existence of God. So, if you know those arguments, then you can say that you know God exists.

Faith, on the other hand, is trust. I have faith that Jesus is God because I trust Him, not because I can prove on my own that He is God. I cannot argue from experience and reason that Jesus is God. There is a point where I either trust him or I do not. A historical study can reveal that Jesus claimed to be God and that he rose from the dead, but I have to have faith in him to believe that He is God. If he is God, then no one is more trustworthy.

Knowledge is like seeing a stack of boxes. I can look at the structure and see how the top box is connected to the ground. I don't have to trust anyone else to know that the top box is grounded in reality because I can see it for myself.

Faith is like having a screen or wall over which I can see a box, but another person is on the other side of the wall. I cannot see how well the box is grounded in reality, the other person can. That person tells me about how that box is connected to the ground. If the person is trustworthy, I believe him that the box is grounded.

Knowledge is what I can see. Faith is trusting what someone else can see.

"Jesus, what is God like?"

"Look at me."

"But you come from a tradition where God is already described in a library of books."

"Yes, I am the fulfillment of that library."

"But you look nothing like the God described there."

"All the time? All of the descriptions?"

"Well, some of the descriptions look like You, but a lot of them look very, very different."

"Can a cup hold a gallon of water?"

"If it is a big enough cup."

"I mean a regular cup. Can a normal, regular, dinner-table drinking glass hold a gallon of water?"

"I think you are changing the subject."

"Trust me."

"No, a normal drinking glass cannot hold a gallon of water."

"God is more than a gallon, and the spiritual maturity of the human race is less than a glass."

"I don't understand."

"People can only receive according to what they are. People only perceive according to what they already know. People only react according to their perceptions."

"So?"

"So, don't expect God to appear kind, loving, and forgiving to people who are angry, hateful, and vindictive. Don't look for a theologically rigorous idea of God to be communicated by non-theologians."

"God didn't write that library?"

"No, but He inspired it."

"If it is inspired, why is it so far off?"

"It is totally accurate in its description of the relationship God has with his people, how they understood Him, and how they heard Him. It must all be seen in light of the new revealed standard."

"What is that standard?"

"I am."

Chapter 11

The Pillar and Bulwark of the Truth

T or F?

1. It is just me and Jesus.
2. Jesus wrote the Bible.
3. Jesus founded the Church.
4. If there were no Church, there would be no Bible.
5. Anyone can interpret the Bible for himself.
6. Jesus entrusted his teaching to the Church.
7. Bad people in the Church proves Christianity is false.
8. The Church is a building.

Papa: I must first fight with shadows, that collection of many and varied sources of your prejudices against me. Every negative comment, every slander, every time someone said that I didn't matter, that I was old-fashioned, that I was bad for society, and that I was said to be a result of greedy attitudes and man-made traditions, every joke, every scary cartoon image have contributed to your gut-level reactions when you hear about me. I do not know them by name, and I do not know when you heard them, but they have almost made me forget who I am. I cannot bring up their charges one by one because they are so vague and baseless. You don't even remember all the specific moments, but they have all added up to a negative association with my name. That is my most imposing opponent.

Despair: No one is good. No one has truth. All authority is undermined by bad actions.

Resentment: Hate those who have abused their authority. Rebel against them and look only at their poor actions.

Hope: But God can use imperfect people. Authority to teach truth depends on God's inspiration, not man's ability.

Ad hominem: A logical fallacy where someone tries to disprove a statement by impugning the character of the person who said it.

e.g. There have been many bad popes. Therefore the teaching of the Catholic Church is false.

e.g. The Crusades. Therefore the teaching of the Catholic Church is false.

e.g. The Inquisition. Therefore the teaching of the Catholic Church is false.

Scientism: Why are you against science?

Church: Excuse me?

Scientism: Why do you not allow people to think scientifically?

Church: I don't know what you are talking about.

Scientism: Really? Everyone knows that the Church is anti-science.

Church: Science? Science is my child. The philosophical groundwork for the scientific method was laid in Christian Europe in the Middle Ages.

Scientism: Then why have you persecuted so many scientists?

Church: Like who?

Scientism: Galileo!

Church: Galileo is my son.

Scientism: Then why did you imprison him for proving that the earth goes around the sun?

Church: I didn't. First of all, he didn't prove that the earth goes around the sun, even though he preached that he did. Second, he was placed under a very comfortable house arrest because he betrayed his friends and people reacted badly. It was a complicated time for my children.

Scientism: But he taught that the earth goes around the sun, and it was your official teaching that the sun goes around the earth.

Church: That has never been my official teaching, and others have taught the same thing without suffering any kind of discipline at all, like Nicholas of Cusa.

Scientism: What about Giordano Bruno?

Church: He was not a scientist. He never made any astronomical observations or performed any experiments. He was a fraud.

Scientism: Then what about... um...

Church: What about the many Catholic scientists who have only been encouraged by the Church? Like Fr. George LeMaitre, the Catholic priest who invented the Big Bang Theory?

Dear diary,

I had the strangest experience yesterday. I had ordered a couch for my very modern apartment. When it arrived, the deliverymen and I unwrapped it, and it was hideous. It had all kinds of ornate patterns and carvings in the surrounding woodwork. The fabric was multicolored with intricate designs and pictures. I had ordered a very plain, stark, mono-colored couch, and this was not it. I was afraid I was going to have to throw the couch away or send it back. Thankfully, one of the deliverymen looked again at the delivery information, and he discovered that he had been holding it upside down. I live in apartment 2, but the couch was supposed to go to apartment 7. The seven had been written in such a way that when it was flipped upside down, it looked like a two.

So, we reapplied what we could of the wrapping, and we sent the couch to apartment 7. I was curious to meet this person who could have ordered such a couch. When the door opened, I immediately began to understand. The couch fit perfectly with the style of apartment 7. Immediately, I recognized the patterns in the wood in the trim of the room and the other furniture. The colors all harmonized, and as I looked further, I discovered that the images and shapes in the fabric were in the wallpaper and paintings on the wall. The entire apartment was filled with unending detail, which seemed to make sense out of the couch. The furniture that made absolutely no sense in my apartment suddenly became beautiful and meaningful in apartment 7. Some of the pieces were very, very old, but different parts of the surroundings gave new understanding to those older pieces. I thought that it would take a lifetime to go through that whole place and make all of the connections between all the pieces of furniture, the ceiling illustrations, the statues, the paintings, and even the woodwork and tiles in the floor; and yet there was a coherence that was immediately evident upon entering the room. Even the music that was playing seemed to "fit."

When I got back to apartment 2, my new, plain, stark couch had arrived. Despite the new couch, I felt sad. My couch, and my apartment as a whole, meant nothing.

Todayism: You are out of date.

Church: Can you clarify your statement?

Todayism: The Church is a relic of the past and is holding society back.

Church: If you mean by "a relic of the past" that the Church dates back to ancient times, then I agree with you.

Todayism: But you are so old.

Church: And...?

Todayism: We need something more up to date and progressive.

Church: Why?

Todayism: So that we can make progress and get rid of old ways.

Church: What is progress?

Todayism: Moving forward.

Church: In which direction?

Todayism: Into the future.

Church: I think that will happen whether you like it or not. How do you know the difference between progress and regress?

Todayism: Just away from the past.

Church: I think that would be the future, and we've been over that.

Todayism: It is just that everything from the past is backwards and wrong.

Church: Does that mean that, in the future, everything from today will be backwards and wrong?

Todayism: No. We are too modern to be wrong. We have learned from our mistakes and the opinions of the Church have been disproven.

Church: When? By whom?

Todayism: Science!

Church: I just finished that conversation. Do we have to do it again?

In the end, there is only one thing that matters for belief: truth. Almost every objections against the Catholic Church turns out to be a logical fallacy or a misunderstanding of what the Church actually teaches. People who reject the Church because She is old are committing the fallacy of chronological snobbery, the fallacy that says we can tell the truth of an idea by its age. People who reject the Church because of some people in the Church who made bad choices are committing the fallacy of ad hominem, the fallacy that says we can judge an idea by some of the people who have held it. Those who reject the Church because she teaches that some people are better than others are missing out on the truth that the Church teaches: the dignity and value of every human being. Those who reject the Church because they think the Church is man-made are missing out on the truth that the Church was founded by Jesus. Those who reject the Church because man cannot usurp the teaching of God are missing out on the truth that the Church's teaching comes from God. Those who reject the Church because Catholics worship saints and statues misunderstand the fact that we ask the saints to pray for us without worshipping them and keep their statues as reminders and symbols of them.

Person: Hey Jesus! I like you!
Jesus: Thanks. I love you.

Person: You know, Jesus, I am so glad that I don't need religion or any of those rules. I am really happy that it can just be me and you.

Jesus: What do you mean?

Person: It's just you and me! We don't need any institutions or churches or priests or hierarchy. I don't need to confess my sins or be admitted to any organization or go through any rites and ceremonies. I don't like that stuff anyway. I can just go straight to the God-man himself, you, Jesus.

Jesus: Well, I guess that is possible, but why are you asserting it so firmly? I am not limited to work in any particular way, but why are you talking about just you and me with such certainty?

Person: Isn't that what you taught?

Jesus: When did I ever teach that it's just you and me? If you love me, follow my teaching.

Person: But didn't you teach that it's just you and me in the Bible?

Jesus: If it was just you and me, there would be no Bible. The Bible comes from the Church. I founded the Church. If you hear the Church, you hear me.

Judge: Order! Order in the court. Will you call your next witness?

Attorney: Yes, I would like to call to the stand Patri Ecclesiae.

Judge: Who?

Attorney: Patri Ecclesiae.

Judge: That's a strange name.

Attorney: Yes, but it is a fitting name.

Judge: Is it really necessary to call Mr. Ecclesiae to the stand? Don't we have the basic documents that we need?

Attorney: Yes, your honor, we have the basic documents, but without this witness we wouldn't know which of these basic documents make up the Bible and which ones don't.

Judge: All right, then, bring him in.

Attorney: So, tell us Patri, give us your testimony.

Patri: I can attest to the presence of the New Testament in the Early Church and the eventual agreement on its canon...

Judge: Thank you! That will be all.

Attorney: But your honor, I think he has more to say.

Judge: Is it really necessary? We have the essential documents, what more do we need?

Attorney: I think we should hear him out because we might not know what else we need. Maybe he has some important evidence we do not even know that we need.

Judge: Well, I will allow it. But tell him to

be brief.

Attorney: Carry on, Mr. Ecclesiae.

Patri: Thank you. I will also testify about the Old Testament canon that was agreed upon side-by-side with the New Testament canon, and the list of books is the same as the Roman Catholics have today. I can also testify to the importance of Tradition in the Church and the teaching authority of the Church to define dogma and authentically interpret Scripture. I can testify to the real presence of Jesus in the Eucharist, the veneration of saints, and...

Judge: That is enough. We don't need all of that. We have the essential documents and we can read them for ourselves.

Attorney: But your honor, if we need this witness for those essential documents, how can we throw out his testimony on these other topics? Either we take all or nothing. If he is trustworthy for the essential documents, then he has to be trustworthy for everything. If he is untrustworthy for everything else, then he is untrustworthy for the essential documents.

Judge: Hmm. That is a good point.

There was once a house with three walls. One wall was a library of very old books, another wall was covered in old family photos, and the other wall contained a select number of books which were beautifully crafted. The select books were only a little older than the old library, but they were more precious.

A renovator came to the house and wanted to keep only the wall of select books. He began by tearing down the wall of very old books, and immediately the rest of the house began to crack and crumble. He wondered why it was already starting to fall apart, but he continued his renovation project and tore down the other wall of family photos. He did not realize that the walls supported each other, and the wall of select books could not stand on its own, and it all came tumbling down.

Jesus promised that the Holy Spirit would guide the Church into all truth. Either the Holy Spirit has guided the Church in all truth, or Jesus was a liar.

If I trust Jesus, then I trust in his promise to lead the Church into all truth. I trust the Church because I trust Jesus. In the words of the Bible, the Church is the pillar and the bulwark of truth. The Bible, the authority of the Church, and Tradition all work together to give us the truth about God, man, and salvation.

I find perfect agreement between what the Church teaches and the results of good philosophy. In fact, whatever good philosophy reveals is affirmed by the Church, and then the Church is able to tell me more about the nature of God, the source of existence, morality, and how to be saved. Faith and reason find a perfect home together in Catholicism. Reason leads me to faith, and faith informs and expands my reason.

Wiseguy: So, you're saying that philosophy and the teaching of the Church line up with one another?

Fool: Well, philosophy deals with reality, and the Church's teaching deals with reality, too. So, they have to agree, don't they? There can only be one truth because there is only one reality.

Wiseguy: But the Church teaches the opposite of so many philosophers.

Fool: Well, the teaching of the Church doesn't agree with all philosophers because not even all those philosophers can agree with each other. The Church's teaching affirms true philosophy, the philosophy that actually makes sense of reality and our experience.

Wiseguy: What about all the other philosophies?

Fool: They are not true.

Wiseguy: You are only saying that because they contradict the Church's teaching.

Fool: No, I don't think so. Those other philosophies are not true because they contradict the data we get about reality. Some of them even contradict themselves.

Wiseguy: Well, the Church requires faith, and faith and reason can't go together.

Fool: Why not?

Wiseguy: Because if we know that something is true by reason, then we don't need faith. But the Church requires faith and even calls it a virtue.

Fool: Oh, ok. I see what you mean. Yes, if we know something by reason, then we don't need faith. But not everyone knows everything by reason, and there are some things that reason, by itself, can't reach.

Wiseguy: Explain yourself.

Fool: Well, someone who can argue for the existence of God knows that God exists, but faith affirms what he already knows. But for people who have not or cannot go through the arguments, they can still know by faith that God exists.

Wiseguy: What about things beyond reason? Doesn't that mean that those things are irrational?

Fool: No. "Beyond reason" is not the same thing as "against reason." "Beyond reason" just means that we don't have the ability to figure out those things on our own. The teaching about the Trinity is one of them.

Wiseguy: But why trust the Church?

Fool: I think we have been through that already.

A Philosophical Sermon

The Meaning of Life

Today, I would like to address a question that is often asked rhetorically, when someone is feeling down and depressed, as an expression of the apparent meaninglessness of life. But, if an answer were honestly and carefully sought, the seeker might find the most wonderful answer possible. To do justice to the asker, we must remember that he does not know in the beginning. At the point of asking, he does not know whether life is meaningless or not, but he ought to remember that it cannot hurt to find out. Truth at all costs.

The question "What is the meaning of life" is asking about this phrase: the meaning of life. There are two main words there: meaning and life. I would like to begin by analyzing each word separately, and then we will put them together again.

First of all, the word meaning. We use this

word quite often, especially when learning some new subject or language. "What does that mean?" "What does this symbol mean?" "What does that word mean?" The main idea is what words, symbols, and signs have a meaning. Words and symbols are not mere ink-marks on a page or pressurized wave disturbances in the air. There is something more to them. They point beyond themselves.

A common mistake when learning a new language is to learn that words from the new language mean something in English. For example, it is a mistake to think that gato in Spanish means cat in English. The word gato in Spanish can be translated into cat in English, and one word can be substituted for the other in the minds of people who know both languages. Instead, the meaning of the word gato is that thing signified by the word, the cat itself, the living, breathing, physical reality to which the word refers. Or the word means the idea of "cat" that I have in my mind. Gato and cat have the same meaning, but one word does not mean the other. A word means something because it points the mind to an idea or an object.

Another sense of the word meaning is applied in cases where evidence is being discovered or presented. For example, a detective may find a wet umbrella at the scene of a crime and ask himself, "What does it mean?" The presence of the umbrella means something, it implies something, it points to something. It is a clue that must have an explanation. The broken chair and the eaten porridge meant that someone had at least been present, and might have still been present, in the home of the three bears.

Now, the other key word in our question is life. I am going to take a specific meaning of this word, a meaning that may not always be intended by the asker, but it will help to be specific at the start. After all, the word life has many different nuances and uses, and vague use of words will yield, at best, vague conclusions. The exact meaning of the word would be best expressed if we added another word to get the phrase my life. Let the seeker seek the meaning of his own life.

I believe that this question can be rephrased and narrowed further to get it to a point that we can analyze. After all, to ask the meaning of my life may refer to mere biological functioning. But I do not think that is the intended meaning. I think it has more to do with existence. By life, I think the asker is referring to his own existence. What does it mean that I exist? Is my life a "tale told by an idiot, full of sound and fury, signifying nothing," or does it signify something else?

Thankfully, we are now in a place where we recognize the terms. Existence. This concept is the whole basis of our philosophy. To be. Being. Remember that we do not exist from ourselves, we rely on something else for our existence. We do not have to exist because it is not part of our nature to exist. The reason we exist is that Being Itself sustains us in our existence. All of this follows directly from the investigations of the preceding pages. My existence, my life finds its reason in the Essence of Existence.

Remember also this basic corollary: Being Itself has a will. Since I did not have to exist, I had to be willed into existence freely; a decision had to be made to create. That decision was obviously made since I exist, and existence can only come from the Essence of Existence. Therefore, Being Itself has a will and is personal.

The meaning of my existence, the meaning of my life is now obvious: the Essence of Existence wills my life.

I would now like to take a moment to introduce an important point. Love is the willing of the good of the other. Real love does not seek gain for the lover, but seeks the good of the beloved, and the basis of all goodness is existence. A thing can have no goodness if it does not exist. Love, therefore, in its most basic sense, wills the existence, the full existence of the beloved. Love wants the beloved primarily to be.

Therefore, if the Essence of Existence wills my life, then I can translate that to mean that God loves me. The meaning of my life is that God loves me. My continued existence signifies first and foremost that I am beloved by God. This is not the result of wishful thinking or religious revelation; it comes from honest appraisal of philosophical principles and processes. Not surprisingly, it matches perfectly with what the true religion teaches us about God and ourselves. God loves us.

However, it is important that we take this conclusion to further conclusions. This sense of saying that "God loves me" is the answer to the question of the meaning of life implies far more than "God likes me" or "God likes to spend time with me." It means that God loves me from the inside, from the very core and center of my being. God does not discover me, inspect me, find me tolerable and make a decision to love me. God is responsible for my very existence each and every moment. Were God to stop loving me, I would cease to exist. This is the fullest, most inexorable sense of the word love, and my life means that God loves me in this very sense. It sounds trite to say that "God loves me" is the answer to the question of the meaning of life, but that is only because we have either forgotten or never learned what it means to say that God loves me.

I cannot do anything to stop God from loving me. Since I am not loved on the basis of my qualities and accomplishments, I cannot ever or in any way make God stop loving me. If I begin to doubt for a moment that God loves me, I need ask myself one question: do I exist? Obviously, I exist. A not-existing-thing could not have asked the question. I think; therefore I am. I am; therefore God loves me.

That also means that I don't have to earn God's love. Indeed, as I become a better person, I realize more and more how much God loves me in an almost tangible way. But I do not have to earn his love at the beginning. Quite the contrary, all of the good that I can do comes from God's love for me. He teaches me to love and gives me the power to love. God is the inventor and the power supply. I can do no good on my own. Indeed, I cannot even exist on my own.

The next conclusion follows from realizing that I am not the only me. If the meaning of my life is that God loves me, then the meaning of my neighbor's life means that God loves him. I ought, then, to love him also. If a person exists, God loves him, and I have no business saying that I love God but do not love what He loves. I sometimes get the impression that people are asking more of an ethical, moral, or practical question when they ask about the meaning of life, as if to say, "What ought I to do?" or "What is my purpose?" Our investigation thus far, then, will be disappointing. But this present paragraph should satisfy them. The purpose of my life is to love. Since I, too, have a will, then I, too, can and ought to love. Every single other human being is willed by the Creator and loved from the very center of his existence. I was made out of love and for love. The meaning of my life is to love and to be loved; this is the "fundamental vocation" of every person, and a man reaches his highest potential in fulfilling it.

From this viewpoint of ethics, all the other virtues follow. A coward cannot love since he cannot act against his own selfish impulses. A fool cannot love since he will not know the good of the other or how to bring it about. A doubter cannot love because he will falter in his assurance that love is the right thing to do. All the other virtues are at the service of love.

This principle that what exists is loved can be extended to all of existence, the whole natural and supernatural world. Everything that exists is loved by God with the love proper to it. What exists is loved, and we humans have a moral obligation to love it, care for it, and sustain it because it is part of our nature to do so. The love at the foundation of our being is the same love at the foundation of every other being.

One more insight. It is a cosmological understatement to say that God is with me. Not only is He with me; He is in me and all around me; He is sustaining every fiber of my being; He is loving me from the inside all the time. God's love is the cause of my existence. It is one of the greatest deceptions of our time that people think they are alone and unloved. If that were the case, they would not exist.

It is important now to realize that, having solved the riddle of the meaning of life, our life is not over. Answering fundamental questions does not put an end to all questions; it only gives us a measuring stick for all our other practical decisions. Life is still to be lived. Challenges will come. Every day will bring something new, and our answers provide a foundation for building a new and fulfilling life. A fully formed philosophy is not a bed for sleeping; it is a sword for cutting through the Gordian knots of life. Knowledge of truth has to do with the intellectual part of man, and man is more than a mere intellect. God loves you. That says it all, and that settles all. Now, go live it.

Why You Should Not Have Read This Book

or What authors and works you should have been reading instead of this

or Where I got my ideas

Beginner

- Plato
- Mortimer Adler
- G.K. Chesterton
- C.S. Lewis
- Peter Kreeft
- Walker Percy
- Stephen Barr
- Compendium to the Catechism of the Catholic Church
- The New Testament

Advanced

- Aristotle
- Étienne Gilson
- Jacques Maritain
- Josef Pieper
- Dennis and Ralph McInerny
- Thomas Aquinas
- Reginald Garrigou-Lagrange
- Stanley Jaki
- The Catechism of the Catholic Church (one of the Catholic Church's two best kept secrets; the other is the saints.)
- The Bible